Population and the New Biology

Proceedings of the Tenth Annual
Symposium of the Eugenics Society
London 1973

Edited by
BERNARD BENJAMIN
The City University,
London

PETER R. COX
Government Actuary's Department,
London

JOHN PEEL
Teesside Polytechnic,
Middlesbrough, Teesside

1974

Academic Press · London · New York
A Subsidiary of Harcourt Brace Jovanovich, Publishers

ACADEMIC PRESS INC. (LONDON) LTD.
24/28 Oval Road,
London, NW1

United States Edition published by
ACADEMIC PRESS INC.
111 Fifth Avenue
New York, New York 10003

Library of Congress Catalog Card Number: 74-6360
ISBN: 0-12-088 340-6

MADE AND PRINTED IN GREAT BRITAIN BY
THE GARDEN CITY PRESS LIMITED,
LETCHWORTH, HERTFORDSHIRE SG6 1JS

Contributors

J. A. BEARDMORE, *Department of Genetics, University College of Swansea, University of Wales, South Wales*

P. R. J. BURCH, *Department of Medical Physics, University of Leeds, England*

P. R. COX, *Government Actuary's Department, Steel House, Tothill Street, London SW1H 9L5 England*

B. M. DICKENS, *The College of Law, 27 Chancery Lane, London WC2A 1NL England*

G. W. DUNCAN, *Population Study Centre, Seattle, Washington, U.S.A.*

G. M. FILSHIE, *Department of Obstetrics and Gynaecology, University of Nottingham, England*

M. J. FREE, *Biology Department, Battelle, Pacific Northwest Laboratories, Richland, Washington, U.S.A.*

B. N. HEMSWORTH, *Life Sciences Laboratory, Teesside Polytechnic, Middlesbrough, Teesside, England*

T. W. MEADE, *Medical Research Council—Department of Health Epidemiology and Medical Care Unit, Northwick Park Hospital Harrow, Middlesex, England*

J. D. POLE, *Department of Health and Social Security, 151 Great Titchfield Street, London W1P 8AD England*

ELIOT SLATER, *Institute of Psychiatry, University of London, Denmark Hill, London, England*

C. M. STEWART, *Government Actuary's Department, Steel House, Tothill Street, London SW1H 9L5 England*

J. M. THODAY, *Department of Genetics, University of Cambridge, England*

CLIVE WOOD, *Linacre College, Oxford, England*

Preface

This volume contains the texts of papers read at the tenth annual Symposium of the Eugenics Society and is the third publication in a trilogy on the general theme of "population". Despite the wealth of recent literature on this topic the previous volumes in this series, *Population and Pollution* and *Resources and Population*, have attained a wide readership and have been well received.

The implications for population structure and growth of those recent advances which have come to be known as the "new biology" have attracted less attention than the problems of pollution and diminishing world resources and the Editors hope that this book will fill an important gap in the literature. Once again we are grateful to those leading representatives of the biological and social sciences who have contributed to this volume.

We wish to record our appreciation of the skilled and unstinting assistance given to us by Miss Faith Schenk and Miss Eileen Walters in the organizing of the Symposium and the preparation of this publication.

On behalf of the Eugenics Society
BERNARD BENJAMIN
PETER R. COX
JOHN PEEL

JANUARY 1974

Contents

General Introduction

J. M. THODAY

Department of Genetics, University of Cambridge, England

Most people are now aware that there are population problems, and more and more people are becoming aware and anxious about the consequences of the development of new biological techniques. Most will also be aware that there are relations between the two. Rather than considering any matters of detail I would therefore like to introduce this volume by raising the question of values.

In such a volume as this, in which aspects of science, new techniques and predictions of social significance are discussed there are always problems of value judgment, and an ever present danger that scientific considerations and value judgments get confounded. It is therefore desirable that we should try and keep our minds as clear as possible concerning the functions of scientific knowledge in these matters, concerning the rôle of scientists, and concerning when it is they stop being scientists and become something else, for of course our role as scientists is only our rôle while we are being scientists. None of us is capable of being scientists all of the time, if only because we have to have values that are outside the realm of science, and it is important that we should be aware, or try to be aware and make clear to others, when we are making statements as scientists and when we are departing from our scientific rôle: otherwise we will surely confound scientific truth, belief and desire, and shall never know how well or ill founded any policies we suggest may be.

For myself I think I have very clear views as to the rôle of science in these matters, but I would not pretend by any means always to be conscious of when I cease to be a scientist and become propagandist, persuader, or what you will, or merely an ordinary citizen, judging as an ordinary citizen should, what, in the light of such knowledge as we have, I think we ought to do.

As I see it we are being scientists while we are using any of those various processes legitimately to be described as scientific method (in or out of the laboratory). We may vary in the success and in the objectivity with which we use these processes, so that our science may be good or bad in various degrees, but this ultimately comes out in the wash so long as discussion is free. We must however remember that we cease to be scientists when we cease to use these processes and start talking about the implications of our findings and expressing our views of what we ought to do with our knowledge.

The processes which we generally call scientific method, are processes for approximating to the truth about the external world—external that is to the scientist. I say approximating to the truth because I am very clear in my mind that Popper's concept of scientific method as a method of falsifying rather than verifying is at the heart of the matter. Scientific method, that is, is a way of rejecting falsehood. Scientific method is, however, something more than that because in the application of scientific conclusions we find we are able to make predictions of the kind "If you do so and so such and such is the likely result", or "If you wish to achieve so and so, such and such is the likely means to achieve it", or "It is not within our concept of the nature of things that such and such a result is achievable". We may put it in a different way by saying that science is our method of determining what means are likely to produce what ends. Except in the special sense that, by using scientific method, we may reach the conclusion that certain ends are not achievable or that certain ends are incompatible with one another, scientific method is not concerned with the ends we ought to desire to reach. Scientific method also involves more than just falsification because it opens up new vistas by producing new means that make possible the achievement of new ends not achievable, perhaps not even imaginable before. But again we cease to be scientists when we start discussing whether these ends *ought* to be aimed at.

These are matters about which there has always been much confusion. But I think in recent years confusion has increased, especially with the increase of ascientific or even anti-scientific attitudes. Perhaps it will help if I put forward three aphorisms concerning such attitudes.

1. The truth or falsity of a scientific statement does not depend on whether it accords with our aims, ends, hopes, fears, politics or ideologies.
2. It is not a criticism of scientific method that we can sometimes demonstrate that the conclusions of scientists are derived from their preconceptions, emotional desires or political attitudes. It is however relevant to the assessment of the degree to which the

scientists used scientific method to reach their conclusions and hence it is relevant to assessment of the scientific validity of those conclusions.

3. The scientific validity of such conclusions is of the utmost importance, because upon it depends, in part, the probability that the means we choose to achieve our ends will actually lead to those ends. Ends certainly cannot justify means that are unlikely to lead to those ends.

This brings me to the essential point of these remarks. We need to try to keep our considerations of means separate from discussion of ends. Our new biological knowledge may influence our ethics, but we must recognize its distinction from our ethics. Scientific knowledge may inform us of the consequences, or some of the consequences of actions open to us, provide us with new techniques (that is new means) of doing various things, and tell us something of the probable consequences of using those means. But we shall surely go astray if we confuse our statements on such matters with our statements about what we would like to do, or about what we think we ought to do.

There is a further related point. It is often argued that scientists ought not to work in areas that might lead to new techniques whose use could have undesirable consequences, part of the argument being that if a technique is available it will be used.

This is a tenable argument, but bristles with difficulties. One difficulty is that the techniques to which pure sciences may lead are unpredictable; for example, I don't think anyone foresaw that work on plant hormones would lead to selective weed killers and in turn defoliants. Another difficulty is that many, if not all, findings are ambivalent, and make possible applications we may think desirable as well as those we may think undesirable. Nor do we necessarily agree about the desirability of particular applications. In addition, the scientist working on a problem may not be the person most likely to see the implications of the findings he may make, though doubtless he should try and draw our attention to the possibilities. But it is not as scientist he will judge them.

Doubtless we shall read of new techniques, or potential applications of new knowledge about the desirability of whose use we may disagree. Let us argue about that, and let us say firmly, if we so believe, that particular applications of some knowledge are undesirable. But let us not confuse such argument with argument about whether or no particular scientific conclusions are valid or not. The two kinds of argument are different, and neither will be profitable if we persist in confusing them.

Finally I think that there is an important additional duty of scientists which they often neglect. We should try to be quite explicit when we consider that evidence at present is such that no firm scientific conclusions can be reached, and that two or more hypotheses are equally tenable. For if there be this kind of uncertainty it behoves us to consider the consequences of our policies in relation to all the tenable hypotheses, not just the one which we prefer.

My general introduction has turned out to be a little sermon, and I have clearly gone beyond my role as scientist. But I hope what I have said may help a little to clarify consideration of the issues raised by this book.

The Creation of Life by New Means

B. N. HEMSWORTH

Life Sciences Laboratory, Teesside Polytechnic, Middlesbrough, Teesside, England

In this paper I shall attempt to review research concerning the production of living things by new methods. Whilst attention is generally confined to experimental zoology, emphasis is placed on aspects which may have a bearing on human reproduction. Throughout the text I will be mainly concerned with procedures which can be regarded as attempts to explore either the developmental potential of the cell and its components in a variety of abnormal environments or attempts to simulate in the laboratory those conditions which currently prevail *in vivo*.

Production of Organic Compounds

The Darwinian theory of evolution postulates the unity of the Earth's bio-sphere. According to Darwin, the higher forms of life evolved from the lower over an extended period in the life of this planet. Fossil analysis indicates that the oldest known forms of living systems may be about 2,000 million years old and study of the oldest rocks, 3,100 million years of age, reveals the presence of stable materials that could be biological residues, namely the simple straight chain hydrocarbons (Calvin, 1969). Over half a century ago Jacques Loeb studied the effect of electric discharges on mixtures of hydrocarbons and suggested that a large number of organic compounds could be formed. However, the first experiments designed with the purpose of testing hypotheses on the origin of life were those of Calvin and his associates, who, in 1951, treated water and carbon dioxide in the Berkeley cyclotron and obtained significant yields of formaldehyde and formic acid. Since then, the majority of papers have dealt with the formation of amino acids and components of nucleic acids from a wide variety of conditions which may be considered pre-biological. Proteinoids have been formed by the thermal polymerization of amino acids; these compounds tend to form microspheres having a diameter in the bacterial range. Energies available for the synthesis of organic compounds under primitive Earth conditions were ultra-violet light, electric discharges, ionizing radiation and heat. While it is evident that sunlight is a principal source of energy, only a fraction of this is in the wavelength below 2,000 Å and could have been absorbed by methane, ammonia and water; however, photodissociation products of these molecules could absorb energy at a higher wavelength.

Next in importance as an energy source are electric discharges and a certain amount of energy was also available from the disintegration of uranium, thorium and potassium-40. Heat from volcanoes provided a comparatively small source of energy. Irradiation of a mixture of methane, ammonia and water by electrons simulating potassium-40 produced adenine, an essential component in DNA and RNA Simulation of primitive Earth conditions in the laboratory has involved passage of these gases through irradiation chambers at 1,000°C, resulting in the formation of several amino acids. Chemosynthesis, due to meteorite impact on the planetary atmosphere, has also been suggested as a pathway for primordial organic synthesis. Simulation of this by firing a ballistic missile into a mixture of methane, ammonia and water vapour is said to lead to the formation of amino acids and a few ultra-violet absorbing compounds, a reaction which is probably due to the intense heat generated momentarily in the wake of the shock wave following impact. One of the primary products in these reactions is hydrogen cyanide and the second is formaldehyde. Using these as starting materials, Ponnamperuma and his co-workers found that a variety of organic compounds could be produced after exposure to ultra-violet light including adenine, guanine and urea. The same form of energy has been instrumental in the production of sugars and purines and in the synthesis of nucleosides, nucleotides and peptides. Ponnamperuma has expressed the view that there is no reason to doubt that we shall rediscover in due course those physical and chemical conditions which once determined and directed chemical evolution (Ponnamperuma, 1965).

Lawless and Boynton (1973) recently attempted to produce amino acids by thermal synthesis from a simulated primitive atmosphere. Using modern analytical methods they found that only six amino acids were produced, which is significantly fewer than indicated in earlier work, and of these compounds only three, i.e. glycine, alanine and aspartic acid, are constituents of protein. Yields from thermal experiments to date are discouraging compared with the discharge experiments which may involve greater energy for synthetic reaction.

Nuclear Transfer

Many years ago it was demonstrated that nuclei from spontaneous frog renal adenocarcinoma (Lucke, 1934) or from renal tumours cultured in the eye chamber of adult frogs will form apparently normal blastulae when transplanted into enucleated egg cytoplasm. A number of blastulae developed into abnormal embryos with recognizable organs and subsequent nuclear transfer gave rise to more advanced embryos (McKinnel, 1962). Improved methods enabled transplantation of nuclei from single cells of frog adenocarcinoma (King and Di Berardino, 1965); however none developed into normal embryos. The technique involving transplanatation of nuclei from embryonic cells into enucleated amphibia eggs, initiated by Briggs and King (1952, 1953) has been extended to involve transfer into non-enucleated ova. Triploids were produced by injection of diploid blastula nuclei into unfertilized Rana japonica eggs (Sambuichi, 1959), and triploid and hexaploid embryos were obtained by Subtelny and Bradt (1960) after transfer of diploid blastula nuclei into activated ova. It appears that polyploidy is due to a union between the introduced diploid nucleus and the resident female pronucleus and studies show that events occurring in the host egg are similar to those due to artificial insemination (Subtelny and Bradt, 1963). Nuclear transplantation studies based mainly on amphibian material suggest that somatic nuclei undergo progressive developmental restriction during embryogenesis. In contrast, it has been suggested that primordial germ cells are developmentally totipotent (Smith, 1965). The capability of germ cell nuclei from Rana pipiens has been examined; nuclei were obtained from primary spermatogonia, secondary spermatogonia and primary spermatocytes. At most, 16 per cent promoted the development of blastulae and none produced normal larvae, where transfer of nuclei from either blastula or gastrula cells proved successful in 77 per cent of cases (Di Berardino et al., 1966).

An important problem in embryology is whether differentiation depends on a stable restriction on genetic information contained in the nucleus, and the technique of nuclear transfer shows that nuclei in differentiating cells become progressively limited in their ability to promote the formation of different types of cell (King and Briggs, 1956; Gurdon, 1960). Gurdon's remarkable experiments showed that over 150 adult fertile toads were produced by nuclei transplanted from endodermal cells of Xenopus laevis, donors ranging from late blastulae to tadpoles (Gurdon, 1962b). The developmental potential of nuclei from fully differentiated intestinal epithelial cells is less; nevertheless 7 per cent have available the genetic information required for the formation of normal feeding tadpoles (Gurdon, 1962a) A fascinating development in this field which has obvious implications involves use of tissue culture. Single nuclei, from epithelial cells grown *in vitro*, were transplanted recently into enucleated unfertilized eggs of Xenopus laevis (Gurdon and Laskey, 1970). Serial transplantation led to the production of metamorphosed tadpoles and adults.

Cell Transfer

Transfer of primordial germ cells between embryos of the same species resulting ultimately in the production of functional gametes was reported by Blackler and Fishberg (1961). Likewise, transfer between sub-species of Xenopus (Blackler, 1962) is successful and in this instance, eggs identical in size and colour with those of the donor were produced by the recipient, indicating specification of these characters by the oocyte rather than by its environment.

Mosaic embryos have two or more cell lines arising from the zygote, whereas chimaeras have two or more cell lines due to a variety of causes such as two separate acts of fertilization, e.g. fertilization of egg and polar body, the fusion of two embryos or the transmission of cells from one twin to another. The incidence of human chimeras is difficult to estimate and this subject has been reviewed recently (Benirschke, 1970). Chimaerism, naturally or artificially caused, is valuable for the study of development. It can be produced by the injection of a cell into the mouse blastocyst (Gardner, 1968) so initiating this condition at a later stage in development compared with that due to the fusion of eggs at cleavage (Tarkowski, 1970) and thus yielding different information. Following injection into the blastocyst a cell may proliferate forming a clone which can be traced through development. This method has been used to study inactivation of the X-chromsome *in vivo* which seems to begin in the 3·5-day-old blastocyst (Gardner and Lyon, 1971) although it is apparently not complete by day 4·5 (Gardner, 1971: Lyon, 1971).

Single blastomeres of rat, mouse and rabbit eggs are capable of development; recently Moore, *et al.*, (1968) have shown that two-, four- and eight-celled rabbit eggs in which all but one blastomere were destroyed could nevertheless develop into apparently normal live young after transfer to recipient does. Survival and development of single blastomeres is dependent on a relatively intact zona pellucida. Single blastomeres devoid of their zona pellucida or single blastomeres placed within a zona pellucida of another egg were rapidly destroyed when transferred to recipient does. (Moore *et al.*, 1969). Removal of one blastomere from a two-celled embryo and its introduction into a new zona, followed by the transfer of both embryos, would produce identical twins which would be invaluable for experimental studies. So far, transfer where a blastomere has been placed in a new zona has failed.

Induction of chimaerism, by aggregation of blastomeres of different strains of mice has been achieved recently. Zeilmaker (1973) fused morulae from different species, namely the rat and the mouse, and reported the aggregation of cellular components leading to the production of a composite blastocyst. Attempts to fuse somatic cells within the zona pellucida of mouse eggs have also proved successful (Lin *et al.*, 1973).

The term parthenogenesis—literally virgin birth—is applied to development that begins without the participation of a spermatozoon in contrast to gynogenesis where activation is induced by a spermatozoon which takes no further part in development. Parthenogenesis can be induced experimentally in some animals, as in the classical experiment of pricking a frog's egg done by Bataillon early in this century. Since then there has been a good deal of research on the induction of parthenogenesis in mammals and a degree of development, occasionally going as far as half-way through pregnancy, has been obtained in mice and rabbits. Theoretically the chances are against the likelihood of parthenogenomes going to term and beyond, because the genome contains many thousands of genes that could mutate to a lethal allele. Because of parthenogenesis these would not be compensated for by normal genes as they commonly are (Austin, 1972). Recently, parthenogenic development of mouse eggs has been induced *in vivo* by electrical treatment (Tarkowski *et al.*, 1970) and *in vitro* by removal of the cumulus cells by Graham in Oxford; in both instances embryos developed beyond the blastocyst stage. Embryos surviving in the uterus to mid-gestation were either haploid, diploid or haploid-diploid mosaics. Triploidy has been induced in mice, rats and rabbits by suppression of the formation of the second polar body; these embryos survived only to mid-gestation.

The first report dealing with the occurrence of gynogenesis was published by Hertwig in 1911. He found that apparently normal embryos were produced when eggs were fertilized by spermatozoa which had received radium gamma-ray doses much higher than levels required to produce abnormalities in all offspring. It was concluded that because of high dosage the genetic material of the spermatozoa was inactivated and played no part in the development of the embryo. The "Hertwig effect" has been demonstrated several times in work involving amphibia and as in other forms of gynogenesis in vertebrates the resulting gynogenomes are usually haploid, although diploidization may occur possibly due to suppression of the second polar body and its participation in subsequent development. Attempts so far to produce the gynogenetic development of mammalian embryos after treatment of sperm *in vitro* with nitrogen mustard have met with little success (Edwards, 1958).

Storage and Maturation of Spermatozoa *in vitro*

Spallazani in 1776 was perhaps the first to report on the effect of freezing temperatures on human spermatozoa although it is doubtful whether the sperm actually froze when exposed to "the freezing cold of winter and its snow". The originator of the concept of banks for frozen human semen was Mantegazza, who in 1886 reported that man's spermatozoa resisted freezing to $-15°C$. No further attempts to freeze human sperm were described until Jahnel (1938) reported motility amongst human spermatozoa surviving temperatures as low as $-269°C$. He indicated that some survived storage for up to 40 days at $-79°C$; storage was not continued beyond 52 hours due to the difficulty associated with holding vaporizing refrigerant. Jahnel raised the possibility that the speed of freezing may be an important factor but he did not investigate this problem; nevertheless he did question whether these procedures might cause induction of congenital malformation. Shettles (1940) confirmed Jahnel's findings to realize survival after reduction in temperature to $-269°C$ and questioned whether the spermatozoa were capable of initiating normal development. Use of rapid freezing, proposed in 1930 by the botanist Stiles, was applied in principle to human spermatozoa by Hoagland and Pincus (1942), who again referred to the concept of a frozen semen bank. Species differences are known to occur to cold shock, namely the irreversible loss of viability due to the rapid cooling of sperm to a few degrees above $0°$ centigrade; ram and bull are very susceptible whereas fowl and human sperm seem little affected (Wales and White, 1959; White and Wales, 1960). The most obvious sign of cold shock is loss of motility which is not regained on warming semen; a variety of structural and biochemical lesions have been associated with this condition (Mann and Lutwak-Mann, 1955).

Prevention of cold shock is achieved by cooling semen slowly from body or room temperature to near $0°C$; apparently the critical range is below $15°C$. Human spermatozoa can survive freezing to very low temperatures moderately well without special treatment, but it was not until the experiments of Polge *et al.*, (1940) and Smith and Polge (1950) involving use of glycerol that the deep freezing of sperm of domestic species became possible. Sherman and his associates studied the influence of the rate of freezing and the protective action of glycerol on human sperm. For the first time these investigators demonstrated that human spermatozoa preserved by freezing were capable of fertilizing an egg and inducing apparently normal embryonic development (Bunge et al., 1954).

Sixteen apparently normal births due to use of frozen human spermatozoa were reported in the United States from 1954–59. Interest in the possible use of human frozen semen banks grew after publication of a nitrogen vapour freezing method, and after the report at the XIth International Congress of Genetics at the Hague in September 1963, where it was announced that normal births had occurred after insemination by human spermatozoa which had been frozen and stored in liquid nitrogen vapour at −196°C (Perloff et al., 1964). Sherman reviewed the implication of these developments (1964).

There is little doubt that a degree of control of human heredity is feasible and it is likely that those who consider that progress in genetic improvement can be achieved through germinal choice will look to frozen semen banks as a means. Further reasons for the development of sperm banks are to remove the objection of irreversibility due to surgical contraception by prior storage of spermatozoa, and for the preservation of certain species.

Although investigation of possible long-term effects are still progressing it has been reported that the physical and mental development of fifty-four children born following artificial insemination, involving use of frozen semen in nine cases, seems normal (Lizuka et al., 1968).

Fertilization and Embryonic Development in vitro

Recent advances have rendered the earliest stages of animal and human development amenable to control in the laboratory. Knowledge from animal experimentation can be extrapolated to man, for example, maturation of the oocyte and fertilization in vitro (Fowler and Edwards, 1973). Successful fertilization of human oocytes in the laboratory stimulated research concerned with the in vitro culture of the embryo during its pre- and post-implantation stage of development; undoubtedly understanding of the control mechanisms affecting these stages will have important physiological, genetic and clinical consequences. The extensive literature in this rapidly developing field makes selection in this review essential.

Stimulation of Follicular Development

Injection of gonadotrophin will induce many follicles to grow and ovulate and progression of the oocyte through the post-dictyate stages is very regular after this treatment. Induction of ovulation by this means is used in cases of amenorrhoea or oligomenorrhoea. It was introduced by Steptoe and Edwards (1970) for those patients whose infertility was due to occlusion of the oviduct and where treatment involved recovery of the pre-ovulatory oocyte, its fertilization and cleavage *in vitro* prior to intra-uterine transfer. Laparoscopy is still the best means for withdrawal of the human oocyte and successful recovery is now of the order of 70 per cent. However, rapid identification of pre-ovulatory follicles which contain fertilizable oocytes still presents difficulty. Excision of ovarian tissue will yield several oocytes and it is interesting to note that the earliest report dealing with their maturation *in vitro* appeared more than 30 years ago (Pincus and Saunders. 1939).

Fertilization

This takes place normally in the ampulla of the oviduct and in the human relatively few sperm reach this site; those which are successful remain active, for two or three days. "Capacitation" of the sperm is essential prior to fertilization (Austin, 1951; Chang, 1951). Ova can be fertilized several hours after ovulation. If maturation of the oocyte begins in the follicle and is completed *in vitro* or in the oviduct then apparently normal foetuses can be obtained at mid-term in various species (Chang, 1955; Cross and Brinster, 1970; Edwards, 1970; Lehman and Dzvik, 1971). Until methods are developed for maturing oocytes more successfully, they must be collected just before or after ovulation if fertilization and embryonic development are required.

Fertilization of Mammalian Eggs *in vitro*

In recent years progress has been rapid. Observations on uterine capacitation led to the use of uterine spermatozoa for the fertilization of rabbit eggs *in vitro* (Chang, 1959). The shift away from uterine sperm began with the report that capacitation could be induced in the hamster by follicular fluid (Yanagimachi, 1969). It is now known that this is dispensable and that capacitation will occur in a chemically defined medium (Toyoda *et al.*, 1971 a and b). Essential requirements for *in vitro* fertilization described by Bavister (1969) have proved effective for the fertilization of human eggs (Edwards *et al.*, 1969; Bavister *et al.*, 1969). It seems appropriate to mention here the range of abnormalities which have been attributed to the ageing of the oocyte. In women, lengthening of the follicular phase occurs spontaneously in various situations, for example, menopause, stress and after use of steroid contraceptives which delay ovulation. Blockage of gonadotrophic discharge in the rat, prior to ovulation, will result in abnormal fertilization and cleavage (Fugo and Butcher, 1966) and an increased incidence of monosomy and trisomy (Butcher and Fugo, 1967). In women there is evidence that when ovulation occurs later than the fifteenth to seventeenth day of the menstrual cycle this is associated with increased abortion or the implantation of abnormal blastocysts (Iffy, 1963; Hertig, 1967). It is only by means of *in vitro* fertilization that the timing of fertilization can be accurately determined and by this means one can study the relationship between the age of gametes and their performance. In primates, especially man, absence of a characteristic oestrus increases the risk of the fusion of aged gametes since coitus may be unrelated to the time of ovulation, unlike the situation in those mammals which are induced ovulators.

Cleavage of Human Embryos *in vitro*
Initial studies were based on media developed for mouse embryos (Edwards *et al.*, 1970); subsequently more complex media supplemented with human or calf serum was used (Edwards *et al.*, 1970; Steptoe *et al.*, 1971). In the most successful media cleavage was regular and several embryos developed into blastocysts. Development of the human embryo to the blastocyst stage in a medium based on cervical fluid was reported recently (Shettles, 1971).

Determination of the Sex of Pre-implantation Embryos
Attempts to separate X- and Y-bearing spermatozoa by a variety of methods have failed to alter significantly the secondary sex ratio (Beatty, 1970). Determination of the sex of the pre-implantation embryo have been based on identification of sex chromatin or the Y body in the nuclei, on use of sex linked enzymes and on immunological methods.

Identification of sex chromatin in excised pieces of trophoblast led to the first successful control of the secondary sex ratio in mammals (Gardner and Edwards, 1968). I do not propose to review possible use of the pre-implantation embryo in clinical studies. Clearly they could be useful for averting the birth of offspring with obvious genetic defects. Excised portions of the embryo could be grown in culture prior to cytogenetic analysis, the remainder being kept temporarily frozen. Fertilized rabbit and unfertilized mouse eggs have developed to term after freezing in protective media. A high proportion of mouse blastocysts survived and developed to term after being frozen at $-79°C$ for 30 minutes (Whittingham, 1971) and successful development after storage at temperatures as low as -169 has been reported recently (Whittingham *et al.*, 1972).

Egg and Embryo Transfer Between Species

Although the first successful experiments involving transfer of eggs were performed by Walter Heape late in the nineteenth century, this work was almost entirely disregarded as a means of livestock improvement or as an approach to aspects of research in reproductive biology until after the Second World War. Egg transfer is now widely used for research purposes and for studies in the larger domestic species. Likewise, transfer of embryos during the pre-implantation stage has met with success (Moor and Rowson, 1964; 1966). Transplantation of fertilized eggs to unmated recipients is widely used in experimental work especially involving sheep and pigs. Egg transplantation has been used as a means for the transport and improvement of "live-stock". Sheep eggs and embryos will survive for several days in the reproductive tract of a rabbit and they have been transported by this means overseas. Pig embryos can be stored in culture media and pregnancies have been obtained in recipients (Polge and Frederick, 1968). Embryos have been transplanted not only at the early stages of development, but later when they have developed into blastocysts (Hunter et al., 1967). Clearly in combination with the storage of embryos in deep freeze these methods will allow an increase in the production of high quality stock and the preservation of species currently threatened by extinction.

Mutagenesis and Embryopathy

It lies beyond the scope of this paper to review the extensive literature which has been published since Muller's discovery in 1927 that X-rays induced mutations in the spermatozoa of Drosophila. It will have to suffice to say that many forms of radiation and a variety of chemicals, including the radiomimetic alkylating agents, have proved to be mutagens. It is very important to gain insight into the activity of drugs and toxic agents against genetic material, for although many embryopathies are due to exposure to chemicals during the formative stages of embryonic life drug action need not be restricted to this period (Hemsworth and Jackson, 1965). Certain alkane sulphonic esters in pregnant rats cause a variety of embryopathies ranging from death *in utero* and congenital malformation, to subtle impairment of gonadal form and function (Hemsworth, 1968; 1969). Thus, depending on the compound used and the time of treatment, control of the fertility of offspring is now feasible.

Only three relevant studies with drugs affecting paternal chromosomes are known and these utilize the criteria of induced heritable sterility and partial sterility in mice. The cause of this embryopathy is considered to be the induction of translocations by the alkylating agents tretamine and methyl methanesulphonate. Biological approaches to modification of genetic material have involved either the transformation of cells by viral infection (Black and White, 1967) or by the nuclear uptake of exogenous DNA by mammalian cells in culture (Robins and Taylor, 1968). These procedures offer scope for further experimentation. Likewise the possible transmission of genetic information from spermatozoa into somatic cells of the female genital tract has been reviewed recently (Reid, 1965).

Possible Developments

It is apparent that the implication of the content of this paper has relevance to man. It is not my intention to recapitulate the views expressed recently by Danielli (1972) except to agree that we are currently on the threshold of one of the most exciting phases in the history of biology, namely the "Synthetic Stage". It may suffice to say that it seems reasonable to envisage that in future the reproduction of man and many animals may be conducted using *in vitro* methods in advantageous conditions. The nature of the objectives which are selected will depend on those factors which motivate man; more than ever before he will have the opportunity to take crucial steps towards controlling the rate and direction of the evolution of his own and related species. Use of frozen germ cells and embryos will enable selective breeding and conservation. Cell and nuclear transfer in combination with mutagens offer scope for greatly increased individual variation as well as for advances in the field of pharmacology. *In vitro* culture of germ cells and their modification by mutagens offers scope for modification of the genotype. Culture of embryonic or adult tissue *in vitro* followed by the transfer of nuclei into enucleated eggs could enable formation of many individuals with a desired genotype.

Acknowledgement

Appreciation is due to Mrs Irene C. Gray for the preparation of the typescript and for the care and accuracy with which she has produced my written drafts and modifications.

References

Austin, C. R. (1951). Observations on the penetration of the sperm into the mammalian egg. *Aust. J. Sci. Res. B*, **4,** 581.

Austin, C. R. (1972). Fertilization. In *Reproduction in Mammals. Book I. Germ Cells and Fertilization*. Edited by C. R. Austin and R. V. Short: Cambridge University Press.

Bavister, B. D. (1969). Environmental factors important for *in vitro* fertilization in the hamster. *J. Reprod. Fertil.*, **18**, 544.

Bavister, B. D., Edwards, R. G. and Steptoe, P. C. (1969). Identification of the midpiece and tail of the spermatozoon during fertilization of human eggs *in vitro*. *J. Reprod. Fertil.*, **20**, 159.

Beatty, R. A. (1970). The genetics of the mammalian gamete. *Biol. Rev.*, **45**, 73.

Benirschke, K. (1970). Spontaneous chimaerism in mammals; a critical review. *Curr. Topics Pathol.*, **51**, 1.

Black, P. H. and White, B. J. (1967). *In vitro* transformation by the adenovirus-S V40 hydrid virus. *J. Exp. Medicine*, **125**, (4), 692.

Blackler, A. W. (1962). Transfer of primordial germ cells between two species of Xenopus laevis. *J. Embryol exp. Morph.*, **10**, (4), 642.

Blackler, A. W. and Fishberg, M. (1961). Transfer of primordial germ cells in Xenopus laevis. *J. Embryol exp. Morph.*, **9**, (4), 634.

Briggs, R. and King, T. J. (1952). Transplantation of living nuclei from blastulae cells into enucleated frogs' eggs. *Proc. Nat. Acad. Sci., U.S.A.*, **38**, 455.

Briggs, R. and King, T. J. (1953). Factors affecting the transplantability of nuclei of frog embryonic cells. *J. Exp. Zool.*, **122**, 485.

Bunge, R. G., Keettel, W. C. and Sherman, J. K. (1954). Clinical use of frozen semen. *Fertil. Steril.*, **5**, 520.

Butcher, R. L. and Fugo, N. W. (1967). Over-ripeness and mammalian ova. II. Delayed ovulation and chromosome anomalies. *Fertil. Steril.*, **18**, 297.

Calvin, M. (1969). *Chemical Evolution.* Oxford: Clarendon Press.

Chang, M. C. (1951). Fertilizing capacity of spermatozoa deposited in the fallopian tubes. *Nature*, **168**, 697.

Chang, M. C. (1955). Fertilization and normal development of follicular oocytes in the rabbit. *Science*, **121**, 867.

Chang, M. C. (1959). Fertilization of rabbit ova *in vitro*. *Nature*, **184**, 466.

Cross, P. C. and Brinster, R. L. (1970). *In vitro* development of mouse oocytes. *Biol. Reprod.*, **3**, 248.

Danielli, J. F. (1972). The artificial synthesis of new life forms in relation to social and industrial evolution. In *The Future of Man*. Edited by F. J. Ebling and G. W. Heath, London and New York: Academic Press.

Di Berardino, M. A., King, T. J. and Bohl, L. (1966). Nuclear transplantation of differentiated male germ cells. *Am. Zool.*, **6**, (4), 28.

Edwards, R. G. (1958). The experimental induction of gynogenesis in the mouse. III. Treatment of sperm with trypaflavine, toluidine blue and nitrogen mustard. *Proc. Roy. Soc., B*, **149**, 117

Edwards, R. G. (1970). Fertilization of human eggs *in vitro*. IX Embryol. Conf. Moscow, 1969. In *Ontogenes*. New York: Plenum.

Edwards, R. G., Bavister, B. D. and Steptoe, P. C. (1969). Early stages of fertilization *in vitro* of human oocytes matured *in vitro*. *Nature*, **221**, 632.

Edwards, R. G., Steptoe, P. C. and Purdy, J. M. (1970). Fertilization and cleavage *in vitro* of pre-ovulatory human oocytes. *Nature*, **227**, 1307.

Fowler, R. E. and Edwards, R. G. (1973). The genetics of early human development. *Progress in Medical Genetics*, **IX**, 49.

Fugo, N. W. and Butcher, R. L. (1966). Overripeness and the mammalian ova. I. Over-ripeness and early embryonic development. *Fertil. Steril.*, **17**, 804.

Gardner, R. L. (1968). Mouse chimaeras obtained by the injection of cells into the blastocyst. *Nature*, **220**, 596.

Gardener, R. L. (1968). Mouse chimaeras obtained by the injection of cells into the blastocyst. *Nature*, **220**, 596.

Gardner, R. L. (1971). Harold C. Mack Symposium. Wayne State University (in press).

Gardner, R. L. and Edwards, R. G. (1968). Control of the sex ratio at full term in the rabbit by transferring sexed blastocysts. *Nature*, **218**, 346.

Gardner, R. L. and Lyon, M. F. (1971). X chromosome inactivation studied by injection of a single cell into the mouse blastocyst. *Nature*, **231**, 385.

Gurdon, J. B. (1960). The developmental capacity of nuclei taken from differentiating endodermal cells of Xenopus laevis. *J. Emrbyol exp. Morph.*, **8**, 505.

Gurdon, J. B. (1962a). The developmental capacity of nuclei taken from intestinal epithelial cells of feeding tadpoles. *J. Embryol. exp. Morph.*, **10**, 622.

Gurdon, J. B. (1962b). Adult frogs derived from the nuclei of single somatic cells. *Develop. Biol.*, **4**, 256.

Gurdon, J. B. and Laskey, R. A. (1970). The transplantation of nuclei from single cultured cells into enucleated frogs' eggs. *J. Embryol exp. Morph.*, **24**, (2), 227.

Hemsworth, B. N. (1968). Embryopathies in the rat due to alkane sulphonates. *J. Reprod. Fert.*, **17**, 325.

Hemsworth, B. N. (1969). Effect of alkane sulphonic esters on ovarian development and function in the rat. *J. Reprod. Fert.*, **18**, 15.

Hemsworth, B. N. and Jackson, H. (1965). Embryopathies induced by cytotoxic substances. In *Biological Council Symposium on Embryopathic Activity of Drugs*. Edited by J. M. Robson, F. Sullivan and R. L. Smith. London: J. and A. Churchill.

Hertig, A. T. (1967). Human trophoblast: normal and abnormal. *Am. J. Clin. Pathol.*, **47**, 249.

Hertwig, O. (1911). Die Radiumkrankheit tierschers keimzellen. *Arch. Mikv. Anat.*, **77**, 97.

Hoagland, H. and Pincus, G. (1942). Revival of mammalian sperm after immersion in liquid nitrogen. *J. Gen. Physiol.*, **25**, 337.

Hunter, R. H. F., Polge, C. and Rowson, L. E. A. (1967). The recovery, transfer and survival of blastocysts in the pig. *J. Reprod. Fert.*, **14**, 501.

Iffy, L. (1963). The time of conception in pathological gestations. *Proc. R. Soc. Med.*, **56**, 1098.

Jahnel, F. (1938). Uber die Wiederstandsfahigkeit von Menschlichen spermatozoen gagenuber starker kalte. *Klin. Wchnschr.*, **17**, 1273.

King, T. J. and Briggs, R. (1956). Serial transplantation of embryonic nuclei. *Cold Spr. Harb. Symp. quant. Biol.*, **21**, 271.

King, T. J. and Di Berardino, M. A. (1965). Transplantation of nuclei from the frog renal adenocarcinoma. *Ann. N. Y. Acad. Sci.*, **126**, 115.

Lawless, J. G. and Boynton, C. D. (1973). Thermal synthesis of amino acids from simulated primitive atmosphere. *Nature*, **243**, 405.

Lehman, A. D. and Dzvik, P. J. (1971). Fertilization and development of pig follicular oocytes. *J. Reprod. Fert.*, **26**, 387.

Lin, T. P., Florence, J. and Oh, J. O. (1973). Cell fusion induced by a virus within the zona pellucida of mouse eggs. *Nature*, **242**, 47.

Lizuka, R., Sawada, Y., Nishima, N. and Ohi, M. (1968). The physical and mental development of children born after artificial insemination. *Int. J. Fert.*, **13**, 24.

Lucke, B. (1934). A neoplastic disease of the kidney of the frog Rana pipiens. *Am. J. Cancer*, **20**, 352.

Lyon, M. F. (1971). Possible mechanism of X chromosome inactivation. *Nature*, **232**, 229.

Mann, T. and Lutwak-Mann, C. (1955). Biochemical changes underlying the phenomenon of cold shock in spermatozoa. *Arch. Sci. Biol.*, **39**, 578.

McKinnel, R. G. (1962). Development of Rana pipiens eggs transplanted with Lucké tumour cells. *Am. Zool.*, **2**, 430.

Moore, N. W., Adams, C. E. and Rowson, L. E. A. (1968). Developmental potential of single blastomeres of the rabbit egg. *J. Reprod. Fert.*, **17**, 527.

Moore, N. W., Polge, C. and Rowson, L. E. A. (1969). The survival of single blastomeres of pig eggs transferred to recipient gilts. *Aust. J. Biol. Sci.*, **22**, 979.

Moor, R. M. and Rowson, L. E. A. (1964). Influence of the embryo and uterus on luteal function in the sheep. *Nature*, **201**, 522.

Moor, R. M. and Rowson, L. E. A. (1966). The corpus luteum of the sheep; functional relationship between embryo and the corpus luteum. *J. Endocrin.* **34**, 233.

Perloff, W. H., Steinberger, E. and Sherman, J. K. (1964). Conception with human spermatozoa frozen by a liquid nitrogen vapour technique. *Fertil. Steril.*, **15**, 501.

Pincus, G. and Saunders, B. (1939). The comparative behaviour of mammalian eggs *in vivo* and *in vitro*. VI. The maturation of human ovarian ova. *Anat. Rec.*, **75**, 537.

Polge, C. and Frederick, G. L. (1968). Culture and storage of fertilized pig eggs. *Proc. 6th Int. Cong. Animal Reprod.* (Paris).

Polge, C., Smith, A. U. and Parkes, A. S. (1949). Revival of spermatozoa after vitrification and dehydration at low temperatures. *Nature*, **164**, 666.

Ponnamperuma, C. (1965). The chemical origin of life. *Science*, May, 39.

Reid, B. L. (1965). Interaction between homologous sperm and somatic cells of the uterus and peritoneum in the mouse. *Exp. Cell Res.*, **40**, 679.

Robins, A. B. and Taylor, D. M. (1968). Nuclear uptake of exogenous DNA by mammalian cells in culture. *Nature*, **217**, 1228.

Sambuichi, H. (1959). Production of polyploids by means of transplantation of nuclei in frogs' eggs. *J. Sci. Hiroshima Univ. Ser. B.*, Div. 1, **18**, 39.

Sherman, J. K. (1963). Banks for frozen stored human spermatozoa. *Proc. 11th. Int. Cong. Genetics.*, 273.

Sherman, J. K. (1964). Research on frozen human semen. *Fertil. Steril.*, **15**, 485.

Shettles, L. B. (1940). The respiration of human spermatozoa and their response to various gases and low temperature. *Am. J. Physiol.*, **128**, 408.

Shettles, L. B. (1971). Human blastocyst grown *in vitro* in ovulation cervical mucus. *Nature*, **229**, 343.

Smith, L. D. (1965). Transplantation of the nuclei of primordial germ cells into enucleated eggs of Rana pipiens. *Proc. Nat. Acad. Sci., US.*, **54**, (1), 107.

Smith, A. U. and Polge, C. (1950). Survival of spermatozoa at low temperatures. *Nature*, **166**, 668.

Steptoe, P. C. and Edwards, R. G. (1970). Laparoscopic recovery of pre-ovulatory human oocytes after priming of ovaries with gonadotrophins. *Lancet*, **1**, 683.

Steptoe, P. C., Edwards, R. G. and Purdy, J. M. (1971). Human blastocysts grown in culture. *Nature*, **229**, 132.

Subtelny, S. and Bradt, C. (1960). Transplantation of blastula nuclei into activated eggs from the body cavity and from the uterus of Rana pipiens. *Develop. Biol.*, **2**, 393.

Subtelny, S. and Bradt, C. (1963). Cytological observations on the early developmental stages of activated Rana pipiens eggs receiving a transplanted blastula nucleus. *J. Morphol.*, **112**, 45.

Tarkowski, A. K. (1970). Germ cells in natural and experimental chimaeras in mammals. *Phil. Trans. Roy. Soc. Lond.*, *B*, **259**, 107.

Tarkowski, A., Witowska, A. and Nowica, J. (1970)— Experimental parthenogenesis in the mouse. *Nature*, **226**, 162.

Toyoda, Y., Yokoyama, M. and Hosi, T. (1971a). Studies on the fertilization of mouse eggs *in vitro*. *Jap. J. Animal Reprod.*, **16**, 147.

Toyoda, Y., Yokoyama, M. and Hosi, T. (1971b). Studies on the fertilization of mouse eggs *in vitro*. *Jap. J. Animal Reprod.*, **16**, 152.

Wales, R. G. and White, I. G. (1959). The susceptibility of spermatozoa to temperature shock. *J. Endocrin.*, **19**, 211.

White, I. G. and Wales, R. G. (1960). The susceptibility of spermatozoa to cold shock. *Int. J. Fertil.*, **5**, 195.

Whittingham, D. G. (1971). Survival of embryos after freezing and thawing. *Nature*, **233**, 125.

Whittingham, D. G., Leibo, S. P. and Mazur, P. (1972). Survival of mouse embryos frozen to $-196°C$ and $-269°C$. *Science*, **178**, 411.

Yanagimachi, R. (1969). *In vitro* capacitation of hamster spermatozoa by follicular fluid. *J. Reprod. Fertil.*, **18**, 275.

Zeilmaker, G. H. (1973). Fusion of rat and mouse morulae and formation of chimaeric blastocysts. *Nature* **242**, 115.

Health Problems in Old Age

T. W. MEADE

M.R.C.-D.H.S.S. Epidemiology and Medical Care Unit, Northwick Park Hospital
Harrow, Middlesex, England

By common usage, "old age" is generally said to start at sixty-five. This is, of course, an entirely arbitrary point (largely determined by normal retiring age) which leads to mis-classification above and below it in terms of an individual's functional capacity, enjoyment of life, and so on. However, in the absence of any biologically meaningful and generally accepted definition that is also easily understood, the undoubted shortcomings of this approach have to be accepted as a basis for discussion.

This paper is not concerned with the population dynamics of old age. To set the scene for what follows, however, we have, first, to bear in mind that the numbers of those aged sixty-five and over have increased about four times since 1900 and that this increase is likely to continue till towards the end of the century; and also that the proportion of the elderly in the population as a whole has risen, though this trend is likely to level out before long. Secondly, life expectancy in those aged sixty-five and over has remained very much the same over the last twenty years or so. What follows is concerned mainly with identifying and caring for illness and disability within this span of life, and very little with possibilities for increasing the span itself.

Our main concern in thinking about health and disease in old age is, of course, the welfare of the elderly themselves. However, this means considering not only their physical and mental problems, but also what confronts those working in the various health and other services who have to deal with these problems.

Table I illustrates this point, not specifically for the elderly, but in a general way; it lists the four leading diseases identified by each of four separate sets of information—data on mortality, hospital discharge

21

TABLE I

Four views of health and disease; leading diagnoses by type and source of information

Deaths* 1971a		Hospital discharges* 1970b		Sickness spells* 1970c		General practice patients‡ yearly (all ages)d	
Coronary disease	143·1	Maternity, etc.	949·8	Influenza	1113·1	Upper respiratory tract	500
Strokes	79·9	Accidents, etc.	505·9	Injuries	842·7	Digestive	300
Lung cancer	30·8	Digestive	492·5	Bronchitis	669·9	Skin	300
Chronic bronchitis	26·1	Respiratory	463·4	Musculoskeletal, etc.	647·7	Minor emotional	250

* In Thousands.
‡ Practice of 2,500 patients.
a. Registrar General (1971).
b. Hospital In-Patient Enquiry (1970).
c. Dept. of Health and Social Security (1970).
d. Fry, J. (1966).

figures, sickness absence figures, and data from general practice. It is clear, for example, that the hospital service sees a rather different picture as compared with general practice or (through sickness absence) industry. As will appear, similar considerations apply in old age, so that simply identifying major diseases from various sources, without also thinking about the practical questions these may pose is of limited value, though an essential first step.

TABLE II

Leading causes of death; % of total deaths by age and sex

	45–64 yrs.		65 yrs. and over	
	M	F	M	F
Circulatory	50·3	36·3	53·7	60·7
Neoplastic	29·1	41·5	20·5	15·1
Respiratory	9·7	7·2	17·1	12·5
Others	10·9	15·0	8·7	11·7
Total	100·0	100·0	100·0	100·0

Registrar General, 1971

Table II shows the major causes of death at sixty-five years and over (and, for comparison, forty-five to sixty-four years). It is perfectly clear that diseases of the circulatory system predominate. This picture would be unlikely to be substantially altered if allowances were made for inaccuracies of certification, known to be frequent in this disease category (and also, incidentally, more frequent as age increases) (Alderson and Meade, 1967) or for the well-known concurrence of several diseases in one patient, also related to age, and not (at present) allowed for in the way mortality figures are presented. These diseases of the circulatory system consist chiefly of conditions resulting from the gradual or sudden blockage of arteries supplying various organs, the heart ("heart attacks"), the brain ("strokes"—where these arteries may also rupture) and legs (peripheral arterial disease) being the most frequently affected—and of high blood pressure and its consequences. In addition to physical illness, arterial disease affecting the brain also causes psychiatric disorders in some 5 per cent of those over sixty-five (discussed in more detail below). Fatal events of arterial disease are often sudden in onset and of short duration—a quick and painless way of dying at the end of what may have been a useful and healthy life. Mortality figures are therefore not always ideal indicators, in the elderly, of the chronic and protracted illnesses which diminish quality of life; on the other hand, arterial diseases are also very frequently chronic and long drawn out, and mortality data may underestimate their burden, because people may be inconvenienced and disabled by them, but die of other causes. At all events, this group of diseases must cause at least as much ill-health in the elderly as any other, and very probably more.

How far arterial disease should be regarded as part of "normal ageing", or how far it is a potentially preventible disease in the elderly, as we believe it may be in middle-age, is an important but difficult and under-investigated question facing research workers. Relationships between coronary artery disease and risk factors such as raised blood cholesterol levels and cigarette smoking become less striking with increasing age, perhaps because those most susceptible have already died, but possibly because the disease process in old age is not identical with that at younger ages. A major impact on mortality from arterial disease is probably the single factor that would lead to substantially greater life expectancy than at present; such a development, however, seems unlikely within the foreseeable future.

Turning to the use of hospital (other than psychiatric hospital) as an indicator of disease, the first point to be made is that over 40 per cent of hospital beds (excluding obstetric beds) are occupied by the 12 per cent of the population over sixty-five (see Arie, 1973). Coronary artery disease and stroke again come high up the list, with diabetes, cataract, pneumonia, gall-bladder disease, arthritis and bone fractures (especially and notoriously of the femur) as other frequent causes of admission (Hospital In-Patient Enquiry, Annual Reports).

Most contacts between patients and doctors are made in general practice. In one North-West London practice, all consultations for each patient (whether at home or in the surgery) are routinely recorded (Levitt and Jarman, 1973), together with the relevant diagnoses. From these records, it is possible to see which diseases are the most frequent reasons for consultations, bearing in mind that many patients consult more than once for the same disease, and also that they may have more than one disease. Using patient-episodes of disease (i.e. counting all the consultations of each individual patient for any disease as one episode), it was found that circulatory, respiratory (excluding influenza) and mental diseases were the three leading groups of diagnoses, each being responsible for over 10% of all patient-episodes in each sex; locomotor diseases (i.e. diseases of the bones, joints and muscles) also accounted for many episodes, especially in women; digestive disease in men featured prominently. Over 40% of all episodes, however, were due to other illnesses and symptoms, often poorly defined.

So far, these glances at health problems in old age have been based entirely on reported sickness—through mortality, hospital discharge and general practice figures. It is, however, increasingly realized that undiagnosed and unreported ill-health and disability in the elderly are widespread. Reasons for this situation vary from unawareness of disease, or belief that it cannot be treated, on the part of the patients themselves, to lack of resources or interest on the part of those responsible for providing service, and to an understandable reluctance to disturb people by discovering conditions for which there is no effective treatment. Surveys of all the members of defined groups are necessary to identify all those with a particular condition, whether diagnosed and treated or not, and the population-based or epidemiological approach to disease in the elderly has been growing in recent years.

A good example is the series of studies in Newcastle on psychiatric disorders in the elderly (for example, Kay et al., 1964). These showed that some 10 per cent of those over sixty-five living at home had organic brain syndromes; about half of these were severe, and about 40 per cent were arteriosclerotic in origin; 1·9 per cent had schizophrenia and allied states, 26·2 per cent had affective disorders and neuroses (in 10 per cent these latter diseases were moderately severe or severe) and 2·6 per cent had other conditions. Thus, 40·7 per cent had psychiatric disorders of one sort or another, and the Newcastle workers estimated that there were fourteen times as many such people living at home as in institutions. Obviously, many of those identified at home had also previously been in hospital, but it is clear that hospital data on their own are of limited value for this sort of problem.

Another good example of a frequently unreported or undiagnosed condition which especially concerns the elderly is low body temperature. Much attention has recently been given to deaths from cold in old people. First impressions that these were the unfortunate but relatively infrequent manifestations of a rather unusual condition have had to be modified by the results of surveys showing that low body temperature is a major and perhaps life-threatening problem in the elderly, especially those in adverse social circumstances. Thus, Fox et al. (1973) found that 10 per cent of a random sample of elderly people living at home had deep body temperatures below 35·5°C (measured by a urine-temperature measuring device). Significantly more people with low deep body temperatures were receiving supplementary pensions than with normal temperatures. In 75 per cent of the homes, room temperatures were at or below 18·3°C, the minimum level recommended by the Parker Morris report on council housing (Ministry of Housing and Local Government, 1961) and in 10 per cent, morning living-room temperatures were at or below 12·0°C. Of the nine individuals with abnormally low morning temperatures (all were above the hypothermic level in the evening) "most were living alone, had no heating in the bedroom, and lacked the basic amenities of hot water in the bath, sink and basin; all were single or widowed; none had central heating . . ." and so on. In summary, this study suggests that while hypothermia itself is not a frequent finding in the elderly, low body temperature, as a potential cause of much discomfort, is all too common; it also indicates very well indeed the contribution that social factors make, and the difficulty of separating them from the purely medical.

Psychiatric disorder and low body temperature have been used as two important and striking instances of the extent to which unreported or unrecognized conditions may exist in the elderly. Visual and hearing difficulties, nutritional problems, the need for chiropody and dental treatment and a number of other examples could just as well have been given—this aspect of the subject is a large and important one.

However, even fairly extensive knowledge of undiagnosed and unreported illness and the ability to treat or care for it still leaves major issues unresolved; for, while domiciliary screening seems to be generally acceptable as a means of identifying such disease, attendance away from home when, for example, special tests or equipment are needed, is less acceptable. In addition, there is some evidence that the elderly may quite often not want to accept treatment for previously undiagnosed conditions—perhaps because their priorities and expectations and those of the people responsible for their welfare do not always coincide. Patient refusal is a not infrequent reason why recommendations on medical care are not implemented in the elderly (Lowther et al., 1970).

So much for a brief and all too superficial review of the many health difficulties of the elderly themselves. What are some of the main problems facing the clinicians, administrators and providers of other services on which the elderly make calls?

First, in many matters, e.g. the use of hospital beds, the elderly undoubtedly make heavy demands relative to their numbers in the population as a whole; this raises a number of questions. Is admission to hospital necessary as often as the figures suggest? Is more extensive treatment and care at home or in day centres feasible?—for if so, not only might there be real economic benefits to the National Health Service as a whole, but in many cases the welfare and personal preferences of elderly patients themselves might be better met. What additional community services (home nurses, physiotherapists, social workers, for example) would be needed for expanded community care? When hospital care is unavoidable, for how long should it be? Are geriatric waiting lists necessary, and what are the consequences of having to wait for admission? What is the outcome of the rapid turnover of patients (see, for example, Hodkinson and Jefferys, 1972) necessary to shorten or abolish waiting lists? There is still often much confusion—sometimes contention—over whether a patient should be admitted to a medical or psychiatric bed, or even admitted at all; the patient caught up in this sort of wrangle has been described as "apt to be seen as a medical problem by the psychiatrist, a psychiatric problem by the geriatric physician, and a hospital problem by the hard-pressed welfare-home attendant" (*British Medical Journal*, 1971). Answers to some of these questions are gradually emerging, but a great deal of research remains to be done.

Secondly, geriatrics is still not a popular career speciality. Many consultant and junior posts in geriatrics remain unfilled; for example, eighty-four out of ninety-nine registrars in geriatric medicine in post in September 1972 were overseas graduates (Department of Health and Social Security, 1973) high-lighting the level of interest of our own graduates in an uncomfortable way. Formal undergraduate training in geriatrics in British medical schools is in its infancy.

Thirdly, and likely to be strongly related to the attractiveness of careers in geriatric medicine, resources are often pathetically inadequate for high levels of care and interest. It is not unusual, for example, for one consultant geriatrician, with insufficient junior medical and other staff, to be responsible for two hundred hospital beds in old and unsuitable buildings (Royal College of Physicians, 1972).

It is certainly true that some progress is now gradually being made in these difficult practical issues. The potential satisfaction and rewards of careers in geriatric medicine are being demonstrated, (for example, Arie, 1973); but there is still a very long way to go before we can be satisfied that the care of the elderly is generally of the same standard that we take for granted in other areas of health.

To end on a cautiously hopeful note, and to provide some justification for this paper being written by an epidemiologist rather than a
geriatrician, the impending reorganization of the National Health
Service involves the appointment of community physicians. If the rôle of
the community physician means anything at all—and there are many
who wonder what it does mean—it is to be able to gather and collate
information in connection with Health Care Planning Teams on just
such pressing topics as the health and health care needs of the elderly;
to estimate the quality and type of services required to meet these
needs; and to advise on the fair and effective allocation of resources.
If, but only if, the workings of the re-organized service really do
turn out to be flexible enough to allow individual districts and their
community physicians to make their local plans in relation to the local
picture; and if sufficient community physicians of high enough calibre
are available, and receive appropriate recognition and support from
their medical and other colleagues, then geriatric medicine in its
widest sense stands to gain a great deal.

Acknowledgements

The views in this paper are entirely my own responsibility. However, I
would like to thank Dr J. O. P. Chamberlain, Dr H. M. Hodkinson
and Dr T. H. D. Arie for a great deal of general help, useful
criticism and suggestions, and Dr H. N. Levitt and Dr B. Jarman for
allowing me to present the data in Table III.

References

Alderson, M. R. and Meade, T. W. (1967). Accuracy of diagnosis on death
certificates compared with that in hospital records. *Br. J. Prev. Soc. Med.*, **21,** 22.

Arie, T. H. D. (1973). Psychiatric needs of the elderly. In *Needs of the Elderly for
Health and Welfare Services.* Institute of Biometry and Community Medicine,
University of Exeter, Publication No. 2.

Br. Med. J., (1971). Leading Article, **3,** 202.

Department of Health and Social Security. Annual Report for 1970 (published
1971). H.M.S.O.

Department of Health and Social Security, (1973). *Health Trends*, **5,** 47.

Fox, R. H., Woodward, P. M., Exton-Smith, A. N., Green, M. F., Donnison, D. V.
and Wicks, M. H. (1973). Body temperatures in the elderly: A national study of
physiological, social and environmental conditions. *Br. med. J.*, **1,** 200.

Fry, J., (1966). *Profiles of Disease.* Edinburgh and London: Livingstone.

Hodkinson, H. M. and Jefferys, P. M. (1972). Making hospital geriatrics work. *Br.
med. J.*, **4,** 536.

Hospital In-Patient Enquiry. Annual Reports. H.M.S.O.

Kay, D. W. K., Beamish, P. and Roth, M. (1964). Old age mental disorders in Newcastle upon Tyne. *Br. J. Psychiat.*, **110,** 146.

Levitt, H. N. and Jarman, B. (1973). Personal Communication.

Lowther, C. P., Macleod, R. D. M. and Williamson, J. (1970). Evaluation of early diagnostic services for the elderly. *Br. med. J.*, **3,** 275.

Ministry of Housing and Local Government (1961). *Homes for To-day and To-morrow.* H.M.S.O.

Registrar General. (1971). Statistical Review of England and Wales. Part I, Tables, Medical (published 1973). H.M.S.O.

Royal College of Physicians of London. (1972). Report of the College Committee on Geriatric Medicine.

What Limits the Life Span?

P. R. J. BURCH

Department of Medical Physics, University of Leeds, England

Population growth has become an issue of public concern and various attempts have been made to forecast trends. If such estimates are to be given a sound analytical basis, explicit assumptions need to be made about sex-specific and age-specific death-rates, as well as live birth-rates and migration-rates. We have to ask, therefore, whether improvements in medicine and public health will continue to reduce death-rates and thereby generate inflationary population pressures. Will research into the various phenomena of ageing—including malignant and degenerative diseases—result in a substantial prolongation of the life span? If this outcome is probable, as some gerontologists believe, should we encourage or discourage investigations into the mechanisms of ageing? Or have we little option but to adopt a *laissez-faire* attitude?

In this paper I review some of the epidemiological evidence for secular trends in England and Wales and make suggestions regarding the biological nature of, and problems of controlling, common fatal diseases.

Trends in Death-Rates and Expectation of Life in England and Wales
A registry of deaths has been maintained in England and Wales since 1841. Figures 1a to c illustrate the sex-specific and age-specific death-rates, for all causes of death, by quinquennia from 1841 until 1970 (Registrar General, 1972). Tables IA and B contain a selection of statistics for the periods 1841–50, 1901–10 and 1961–70, together with the percentage decline in rates from one period to to the next.

Certain broad features call for comment. Apart from occasional excursions such as those associated with the two World Wars, age-specific death-rates have generally declined over the period 1841–1970, although the extent of the fall has been slight in the highest age groups. The steep fall in death-rates in the lowest age-groups that occurred

31

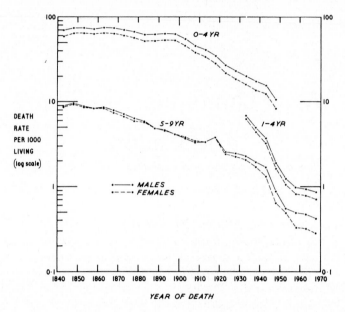

FIG. 1a. Trends in sex-specific and age-specific death-rates, all causes of death, England and Wales, by quinquennia Ages under 10, 1841–1970 (Registrar General, 1972).

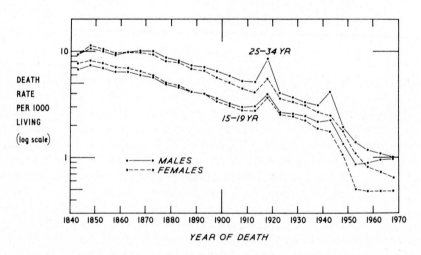

FIG. 1b As for Fig. 1a. Age groups 15–19 and 25–34.

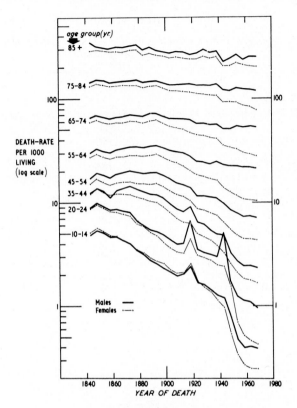

FIG. 1c. As for Fig. 1a. Adult age groups and 10–14 yr.

after 1945 has more or less flattened out over the past ten years, particularly at 10–14 and 15–19 years of age. By contrast, for age-groups above sixty-four years, the gradual fall in death-rates has continued since 1900.

Inevitably, the large changes in age-specific death-rates in children, especially during this century, have lead to pronounced increases in the expectation of life at birth (Fig. 2). However, the growth of the population shows no simple connexion with expectation of life at birth. Figure 3 shows the period 1840 to 1900 to have been one of rapid expansion of population, although death rates (Fig. 1) remained fairly static or declined slightly. The rate of expansion of the population declined after 1914 although the expectation of life at birth increased markedly.

TABLE IA

Secular change in age-specific death-rates. England and Wales. Selected age-groups, males

Age group	1841–50	1901—10		1961—70	
year	Deaths per 1,000 per year	Deaths per 1,000 per year	(Per cent of 1841–50 rate)	Deaths per 1,000 per year	(Per cent of 1901–10 rate)
Under 1*	167	140	(84)	22	(16)
5–9	9·17	3·50	(38)	0·45	(13)
15–19	7·05	3·09	(44)	0·95	(31)
25–34	9·94	5·57	(56)	1·05	(19)
45–54	18·2	16·2	(89)	7·24	(45)
65–74	67·5	64·8	(96)	53·9	(83)
85 and over	312·3	279·2	(89)	254·6	(91)

From Registrar General (1972).
* Infant mortality defined as deaths per 1,000 live births.

TABLE IB

Secular change in age-specific death-rates. England and Wales. Selected age-groups, females

Age group	1841–50	1901–10		1961–70	
year	Deaths per 1,000 per year	Deaths per 1,000 per year	(Per cent of 1841–50 rate)	Deaths per 1,000 per year	(Per cent of 1901—10 rate)
Under 1*	137	114	(83)	17	(15)
5–9	8·90	3·61	(41)	0·30	(8)
15–19	7·89	2·89	(37)	0·38	(13)
25–34	10·6	4·74	(45)	0·68	(14)
45–54	16·0	12·5	(78)	4·37	(35)
56–74	61·0	53·9	(88)	28·8	(53)
85 and over	293·3	250·3	(85)	204·7	(82)

From Registrar General (1972).
* Infant mortality as deaths per 1,000 live births.

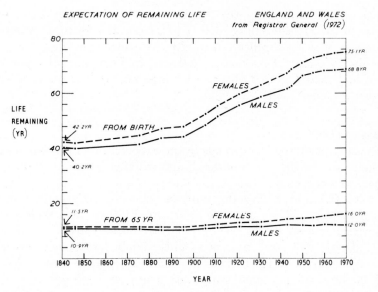

FIG. 2 Change in expectation of remaining life, England and Wales, 1841–1970 (Registrar General, 1972). Upper curves: expectation of life from birth. Lower curves: expectation of remaining life at 65 years of age.

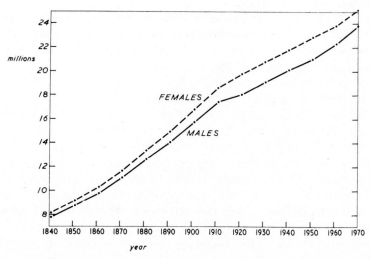

FIG. 3. Growth of population, England and Wales, 1841–1970 (Registrar General, 1972).

Particularly noteworthy from the viewpoint of this paper is the small change in the expectation of further life, especially for men, when the age of sixty-five has been attained. In 1841 this expectation was 10·9 years for men and 11·5 years for women: in 1970, the corresponding values had increased to 12·0 years for men and 16·0 years for women (Registrar General, 1972).

Causes of Death

In assessing possible future trends in the expectation of life, we need to consider the current causes of death and whether mortality from each is likely to increase, decrease, or remain constant.

Tables IIA and B give the numbers of deaths, by certain broad categories of cause, sex and age group, in England and Wales, 1970 (Registrar General, 1972). We see that the broad category "Infective and Parasitic Diseases" is now of only minor importance. Overall, these diseases—perhaps in principle eradicable—were responsible in 1970 for only 0·7 per cent of all male deaths and 0·5 per cent of all female deaths. However, the official category "Infective and Parasitic Diseases" is somewhat misleading. It does not include, for example, deaths from influenza, or viral or bacterial pneumonia: these come under "Diseases of the Respiratory System". Oncogenic viruses might be involved in the pathogenesis of certain malignant diseases and it is claimed by some that "slow viruses" might cause various non-malignant diseases such as multiple sclerosis and systemic lupus erythematosus.

From 30–59 years, deaths from "Neoplasms" (mainly carcinomas) made the largest single contribution to mortality among women. From 60 years and above in women, and from 40 years and above in men, deaths from "Diseases of the Circulatory System" were the most important single broad category. Above 70 years, they constituted an absolute majority of all deaths among both sexes.

In passing, we should note the relative importance of "Accidents, etc." in the early years. At 15–19 years, deaths in this category accounted for 64·6 per cent of all male deaths and 44·7 per cent of all female deaths (about 70 per cent of these deaths in this age group resulted from "Motor Vehicle Traffic Accidents"), but above the age of 60 years, "Accidents, etc." contributed only 1·5 to 3 per cent of all deaths, depending on sex and age group. Hence, even if all such deaths could be eliminated (the category includes suicides) the effect on the average expectation of life at 60 years of age would be small.

TABLE IIA

Deaths by cause, sex and age-group. England and Wales, 1970

Age group	All causes		"Infective and parasitic diseases"		"Neoplasms"	
	M	F	M	F	M	F
			%	%	%	%
0–4	9,584	7,009	428 (4·5)*	317 (4·5)	200 (2·1)	150 (2·1)
5–9	816	538	25 (3·1)	30 (5·6)	153 (18·8)	113 (21·0)
10–14	649	401	20 (3·1)	13 (3·2)	121 (18·6)	107 (26·7)
15–19	1,551	570	19 (1·2)	15 (2·6)	166 (10·7)	75 (13·2)
20–29	3,271	1,645	43 (1·3)	43 (2·6)	465 (14·2)	337 (20·5)
30–39	3,951	2,629	47 (1·2)	40 (1·5)	814 (20·6)	975 (37·1)
40–49	12,969	8,812	158 (1·2)	100 (1·1)	3,174 (24·5)	4,142 (47·0)
50–59	35,752	20,104	319 (0·9)	178 (0·9)	10,309 (28·8)	8,739 (43·5)
60–69	80,681	47,066	522 (0·6)	255 (0·5)	22,295 (27·6)	14,103 (30·0)
70–79	86,511	85,003	400 (0·5)	233 (0·3)	18,512 (21·4)	15,166 (17·8)
80+	57,318	108,364	153 (0·3)	197 (0·2)	7,027 (12·3)	9,933 (9·2)
All ages	293,053	282,141	2,134 (0·7)	1,391 (0·5)	63,236 (21·6)	53,840 (19·1)

From Registrar General (1972).

* Figures in parenthesis represent per cent of deaths from all causes, by sex and age-group.

TABLE IIB

Deaths by cause, sex and age-group. England and Wales, 1970

Age group	"Diseases of circulatory system" M %	F %	"Diseases of respiratory system" M %	F %	"Accidents, poisonings and violence (external cause)" M %	F %
0–4	74 (0·8)	69 (1·0)	1,711 (17·9)	1,252 (17·9)	698 (7·3)	452 (6·4)
5–9	16 (2·0)	15 (2·8)	70 (8·6)	73 (13·6)	369 (45·2)	143 (26·6)
10–14	17 (2·6)	25 (6·2)	57 (8·8)	47 (11·7)	286 (44·1)	94 (23·6)
15–19	70 (4·5)	40 (7·0)	91 (5·9)	48 (8·4)	1,002 (64·6)	255 (44·7)
20–29	277 (8·5)	172 (10·5)	173 (5·3)	154 (9·4)	1,888 (57·7)	514 (31·2)
30–39	1,156 (29·3)	504 (19·2)	267 (6·8)	212 (8·1)	1,190 (30·1)	442 (16·8)
40–49	6,141 (47·4)	2,234 (25·4)	986 (7·6)	702 (8·0)	1,443 (11·1)	647 (7·3)
50–59	17,679 (49·4)	6,660 (33·1)	3,676 (10·3)	1,775 (8·8)	1,633 (4·6)	960 (4·8)
60–69	39,489 (48·9)	22,206 (47·2)	12,408 (15·4)	5,039 (10·7)	1,684 (2·1)	1,362 (2·9)
70–79	44,270 (51·2)	49,329 (58·0)	16,712 (19·3)	10,977 (12·9)	1,324 (1·5)	2,070 (2·4)
80+	32,174 (56·1)	68,453 (63·2)	12,216 (21·3)	17,503 (16·2)	1,160 (2·0)	3,085 (2·8)
All ages	141,363 (48·2)	149,707 (53·1)	48,367 (16·5)	37,782 (13·4)	12,677 (4·3)	10,024 (3·6)

From Registrar General (1972).

Degenerative and Malignant Diseases

The above review shows that, in medically-advanced countries such as England and Wales, the average duration of life is now dominated by the impact on the elderly of the degenerative and malignant diseases. Any appreciable extension of the life span would require the prevention, cure, or delay of these diseases.

What are the prospects of achieving such objectives? If a poll of experts were to be conducted, the answers to this question would probably reflect general beliefs about the causes of diseases of old age. From the medical literature it is easy to gain the impression that most investigators are environmentalists of one form or another, although many gerontologists emphasize endogenous rather than exogenous causes of ageing. In the USA, many oncologists believe that most or all cancers are "caused" by horizontally- or vertically-transmitted viruses. A preoccupation with chemical carcinogens exists in this country and it has been alleged that some 80 per cent of cancers are caused in this way. Physical agents, such as ultra-violet and ionizing radiations, can cause various malignant diseases.

Although, under experimental and abnormal environmental conditions, various physical, chemical and biological agents can undoubtedly induce malignant and other fatal diseases, their contribution to death-rates in the population at large, as recorded by the Registrar General, cannot readily be estimated. In the case of physical and chemical agents, "dose-response" relations become notoriously uncertain and difficult to estimate at low doses and low dose-rates.

According to The Royal College of Physicians (1971), "authoritative committees and commissions" in many countries have all concluded that lung cancer is "almost entirely due to cigarette smoking". The same habit is also said to enhance the risk of dying from chronic bronchitis, emphysema, coronary heart disease, and cancers of the mouth, larynx, oesophagus, bladder and pancreas (Royal College of Physicians, 1971). The association between smoking and coronary heart disease is of special concern because of the enormous number of deaths attributed to this condition.

In view of the great increase in cigarette consumption during this century (Fig. 4) the steady decline since 1900 in age-specific death-rates, seen in Fig. 1c, is somewhat surprising. Perhaps the fatal effects of smoking have been more than counterbalanced by advances in public health and medicine? If that is so, it is even more curious that in the post–1920 period, during which women have become increasingly heavy consumers of cigarettes (Fig. 4), the decline in their death-rates (Fig. 1c) has been steeper than men. During the period

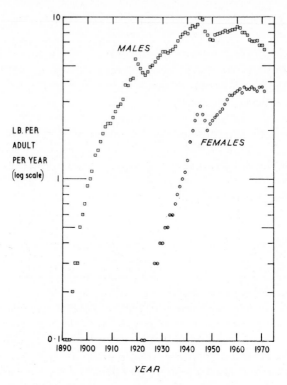

LB. PER
ADULT
PER YEAR
(log scale)

FIG. 4. Consumption of manufactured cigarettes (lb. per adult male, or female, per year) in the United Kingdom in relation to calendar year (Todd, 1972).

when men were acquiring the habit of cigarette smoking and women had not started—that is, about 1891 to 1921 (Fig. 4)—the trends of age-specific death-rates in the two sexes ran almost parallel (Fig. 1c). Thus, when we consider all causes of death, we find no correlation with the secular change in sex-specific cigarette consumption.

Is it conceivable that the many "authoritative committees and commissions" could be mistaken about the significance of the associations between various disorders and cigarette smoking? Several investigators have inclined to a different interpretation (Berkson, 1955; Fisher, 1959; Eysenck, 1965; Thomas, 1968; Rosenblatt, 1969; Friberg, et al. 1973; Thomas, Fargo and Enslein, 1970; Yerushalmy, 1971; Seltzer, 1972a, b, 1973; Stell, 1972; Burch, 1972, 1973).

Critics have suggested that genetic factors might: (i) incline a person to smoke; and (ii) predispose him or her to certain diseases. Numerous investigations support (i) and (ii) separately. It then follows that observed associations between, say, cigarette smoking and particular diseases, might arise from associations between the predisposing genes. A pure "constitutional" theory would attribute the entire association to genetic factors and none to the causal action of cigarette smoke.

In principle, studies of monozygotic and dizygotic twin pairs discordant for smoking habits can distinguish, at a level limited only by numbers, between causal, constitutional and combined hypotheses. The twin studies of Cederlöf et al. (1969) make it clear that both smoking and genetic factors are causally implicated in the pathogenesis of prolonged cough and morbidity from chronic bronchitis. However, the same source of evidence fails to support the hypothesis that cigarette smoking causes an increase in general mortality (Friberg et al., 1973). The data for general mortality and for "cigarette-associated-diseases" are consistent with a "pure" constitutional hypothesis. Negative associations between cigarette smoking on the one hand and, for example, Parkinson's disease and neoplasms of the central nervous system on the other (Choi et al., 1970), can also be accounted for in constitutional terms. Such negative associations are attributed to negative associations between the predisposing genes rather than the therapeutic or prophylactic effects of tobacco. For these and many other reasons, the strident claims regarding the fatal action of cigarette smoking should be treated with reserve.

Other environmentalists seek to incriminate dietary factors, such as refined carbohydrates, animal fats and soft water, in the pathogenesis of circulatory diseases. Pollution and ion depletion of the atmosphere have, of course, been held responsible for various respiratory diseases.

In my view, the rôle of physical and chemical environmental factors in the pathogenesis of fatal diseases of old age tends to be exaggerated. Few investigations in this field are free from potential errors of selection bias. Thus, cigarette smokers, ex-smokers, sweet-eaters, etc., are almost invariably self-selected. In principle, genetic factors might always be responsible at least in part, both for a particular habit and for predisposition to the disease under investigation. Special precautions are necessary to overcome such potential bias and the overall evidence needs to be carefully scrutinized for internal consistency (Fisher, 1959; Yerushalmy, 1971). In considering the association of cigarette smoking with coronary heart disease, lung cancer and overall mortality it is becoming increasingly clear that the potential bias is actual bias (Fisher, 1959; Friberg et al., 1973; Seltzer, 1972a, b; Burch, 1972, 1973).

Aetiology and Pathogenesis of Malignant and Degenerative Disease: Theory

Over the past decade my collaborators and I have paid special attention to certain quantitative characteristics of particular diseases: their age-dependence, and the systematics of the anatomical distribution of lesions. From our studies, and a wide range of other evidence, we have formulated a unified theory of growth and disease. Insofar as the theory relates to disease, it can be regarded as a modification of Sir Macfarlane Burnet's "forbidden clone" theory of autoimmunity (Burnet, 1959, 1965, 1970).

Both theories hold that many age-dependent diseases are initiated by rather few, or only one, random somatic mutation in a "central" system. However, whereas Burnet believes that the normal rôle of the "central system" in which the somatic mutations occur is that of classical immunity, we deduce that the normal, or physiological, function of this system is the control and co-ordination of the growth of the organism (Burwell, 1963; Burch and Burwell, 1965; Burch, 1968, 1970; Burch and Rowell, 1970; Burch et al., 1971; Jackson et al., 1973). We call those numerous diseases that are initiated by spontaneous somatic gene mutations in cells of the central system of growth-control, *autoaggressive*. Our general conclusions regarding the aetiology and pathogenesis of autoaggressive diseases can be outlined as follows.

1. In ordinary environments, a specific autoaggressive disease occurs only in those persons who have a specific genetic predisposition to the disease.

2. The disease process is initiated when r specific random somatic mutations have occurred in each of n specific and independent growth-control stem cells.

3. In the non-infectious and non-allergic diseases, each of the n specifically-mutant growth-control stem cells propagates a "forbidden clone" of pathogenic descendant cells. Each descendant cell carries the mutational defects of its progenitor.

4. In the classical infectious and allergic diseases, pathogenic forbidden clones develop only in the presence of the specific infectious or allergic agent. In their absence, or in a suitably immunized person, an endogenous defence mechanism based on immunoglobulins prevents the development of pathogenic forbidden clones.

5. Cells of forbidden clones, or their secreted humoral macromolecules, attack cells of the target tissue that carry complementary "recognition" macromolecules. We call this phase of the disease

process *development*. The end effects are as varied as disease itself. They may entail the abnormal proliferation of target cells (hyperplasia, neoplasia), destruction (baldness, periodontal disease, osteoporosis, etc.), or subtler disturbances of normal cellular function and metabolism.

6. The duration of the latent period from initiation to onset may be affected by extrinsic agents such as infective microorganisms, and by severe mental stress. For one general class of autoaggressive disease, the average duration of the the latent period in women is double that in men: for the other general class, the average duration is the same in both sexes. In the classical infectious diseases, the influence of the invading microorganism is qualitative: the latent period is comparable to the induction period when microorganisms successfully invade the host, but indefinitely long in their absence. When the microorganism invades a host without a potentially pathogenic forbidden clone, the infectious disease fails to develop and we have the well known *carrier state*.

7. The target cells of an autoaggressive attack may be located at one, or multiple, anatomical locations depending on genetic factors.

Age-Dependence of Fatal Diseases

Because somatic gene mutation is a random process and because the average rate of each specific somatic mutation appears to be constant from around birth to the onset of disease, the above theory enables the age-dependence of autoaggressive disease to be described mathematically in terms of stochastic equations (Burch, 1966, 1968). Figures 5 to 14 illustrate the age-dependence of a few of the major malignant and degenerative diseases. They show the kind of agreement that is commonly found between observations (represented for simplicity by points, rather than histograms), and the curves, based on the theoretical stochastic equations.

All the data for cancer of the prostate (Figs. 5 to 8), fit the same basic stochastic equation, with $n = 3$, $r = 5$, although rates in Japan are only about one tenth of those in the Western countries. The large differences in rates derive almost entirely from S, the proportion of the male population that is at risk with respect to recorded death (or onset) from cancer of the prostate. If diagnostic levels in Japan and the Western countries are comparable—and accurate—calculated values of S will give the proportion of each male population that is genetically predisposed to fatal cancer of the prostate.

The overall age-pattern for cancer of the ovary (Figs. 9 to 11), requires a minimum of two stochastic equations for its description. I

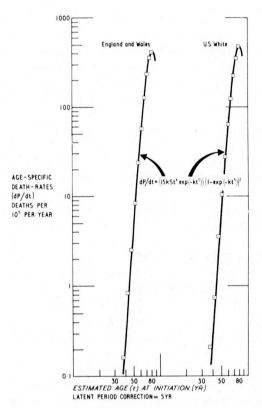

Fig. 5. Cancer of prostate 1960–63. From the model described in the text and elsewhere (Burch, 1966, 1968), it can be shown that, provided certain conditions hold, the age-specific prevalence, P_t, of a non-fatal initiated autoaggressive disease is given by: $P_t = S\{1\text{-}\exp(\text{-}kt^t)\}^n$. Provided diagnosis is accurate, the value of S calculated from age-prevalence statistics defines the proportion of the population, specific for sex or chromosomal constitution where necessary, that is genetically predisposed to the disease. The kinetic constant k is defined as Lm^r, where L is the number of growth-control stem cells at somatic mutational risk in each of the n sets of cells at risk and m is the average rate of somatic mutation of each of the r genes at risk, per cell at risk, per year. If certain additional requirements are satisfied, age-specific initiation rates, dP/dt, of fatal diseases are given by the first derivative of the age-prevalence equation: $dP/dt = \{nrkStr^{-1}\exp(\text{-}kt^r)\}\{1\text{-}\exp(\text{-}kt^r)\}^{n-1}$.

In this figure age-specific mortality statistics for cancer of the prostate (Segi and Kurihara, 1966) are fitted to the equation in which $n = 3$, $r = 5$. For the England and Wales data, 1960–63 (left panel), $k = 3\cdot9 \times 10^{-10}\text{yr}^{-5}$, $S = 1\cdot1 \times 10^{-1}$; for the U.S. White data, 1960–63, $k = 3\cdot7 \times 10^{-10}\text{yr}^{-5}$, $S = 1\cdot3 \times 10^{-1}$.

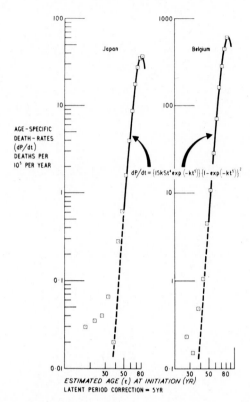

Fig. 6. As for Fig. 5. Cancer of prostate 1960–63. Data for Japan, 1960–63 (left panel), and Belgium, 1960–63 (right panel) (Segi and Kurihara, 1966). Note that the ordinate scale for Japanese death-rates is displaced downwards by a factor of 10 relative to the scale for Belgian death-rates. The following parameters are used to fit the data: Japan, $k = 4\cdot8 \times 10^{-10} \mathrm{yr}^{-5}$, $S = 9\cdot9 \times 10^{-3}$; Belgium, $k = 3\cdot7 \times 10^{-10} \mathrm{yr}^{-5}$, $S = 1\cdot6 \times 10^{-1}$.

conclude that two genetically-distinctive groups (at least) are predisposed to this disease. Again, rates for the late-onset group in Japan are much lower than the corresponding ones in the Western countries but the same basic stochastic equations, with the same values of n and r, fit the data.

Figure 12 reveals one of the main reasons for the greater average longevity of women. Acute myocardial infarction (left panel) is the most important single (detailed) cause of death in England and Wales. The average latent period between initiation and death is about ten years in men, but some twenty years in women. Female advantages of around 2·5 years are seen in the very steeply age-dependent disease,

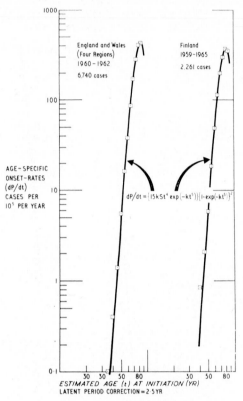

AGE–SPECIFIC
ONSET–RATES
(dP/dt)
CASES PER
10^5 PER YEAR

$$dP/dt = \{15kSt^4 \exp(-kt^5)\}\{1-\exp(-kt^5)\}^2$$

England and Wales
(Four Regions)
1960–1962
6,740 cases

Finland
1959–1965
2.261 cases

ESTIMATED AGE (t) AT INITIATION (YR)
LATENT PERIOD CORRECTION = 2·5 YR

FIG. 7. Registry data for the onset of cancer of prostate (Doll et al., 1966; Doll et al., 1970) require smaller latent period corrections than those needed to convert death-rates to initiation-rates. The latent period corrections in Figs 5 and 6 (mortality data) is 5 years; in Figs 7 and 8 (registry data for onset) it is 2·5 yr. Registry data for England and Wales (4 regions) 1960–62, are fitted by $k = 3·9 \times 10^{-10}\text{yr}^{-5}$, $S = 1·1 \times 10^{-1}$. (These values are the same as those used to fit the mortality data in Fig. 5, for the whole of England and Wales, 1960–63.) The Finnish data, 1959–65 (right panel) are fitted to $k = 4·5 \times 10^{-10}\text{yr}^{-5}$, $S = 1·0 \times 10^{-1}$.

arteriosclerosis (Fig. 12 right panel), and also in cerebral haemorrhage and cerebral thrombosis (Fig. 14).

Figure 13 shows age-specific death-rates for "coronary artery disease"—roughly equivalent to "acute myocardial infarction" in Fig. 12—in relation to the smoking habits of US male veterans (Kahn, 1966). These data suggest the hypothesis that the rate of initiation of the disease is independent of smoking status, but that the latent period between the end of initiation and death is inversely connected with the rate of smoking. This inverse relation might result from causal and/or

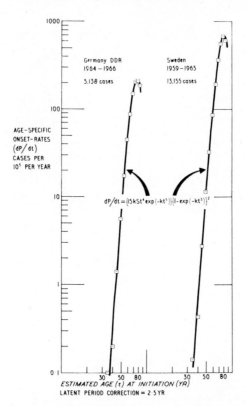

Fig. 8. As for Fig. 7. The onset-rates for Germany D.D.R. 1964–66 (left panel) are fitted with
$k = 5\cdot2 \times 10^{-10}\text{yr}^{-5}$, $S = 5\cdot7 \times 10^{-2}$; Swedish registry data, 1959–65, are fitted by
$k = 4\cdot5 \times 10^{-10}\text{yr}^{-5}$, $S = 1\cdot8 \times 10^{-1}$.

constitutional factors (Burch, 1972). Recent evidence (Friberg *et al.*, 1973; Seltzer, 1973), favours the constitutional rather than causal or combined hypotheses. In other words genetic factors help to determine the average duration of the latent period and these are associated with genes that predispose to certain forms of smoking.

Among the various findings from our studies of the age-dependence of well-defined diseases, fatal and non-fatal, one of the most striking is the high degree of invariance in the values of the parameters n and r that describe the *shapes* of age-patterns. Generally, these are independent of calendar year, country and continent. This large measure of invariance and independence of environment suggests that n and r are determined by intrinsic, biological factors.

In diseases such as Huntington's chorea, the levels, described by S,

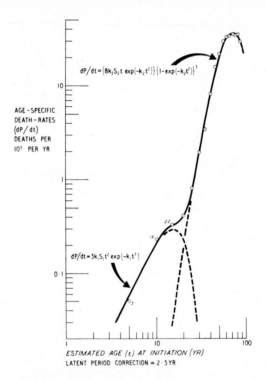

FIG. 9. Age-specific death-rates from malignant neoplasms of the ovary, Fallopian tube and broad ligament, England and Wales, 1960–63 (Segi and Kurihara, 1966). Numbers alongside points represent number of deaths. Two distinctive groups can be discerned. Death-rates for the early onset group are fitted to the general equation (see caption for Fig. 5.), in which $n = 1$, $r = 3$ and with $k_1 = 1\cdot77 \times 10^{-4}\text{yr}^{-3}$ and $S_1 = 4\cdot4 \times 10^{-5}$. The late-onset group is described by $n = 4$, $r = 2$, $k_2 = 3\cdot3 \times 10^{-4}\text{yr}^{-2}$, $S_2 = 2\cdot1 \times 10^{-2}$.

are determined entirely by the frequency of predisposing genes. But in the classical infectious diseases, the calculated value of S may change by an enormous factor, from month to month and year to year, in the same population. The interpretation of S has then to take into account (a) the proportion of the population that is infected and (b) the proportion with pathogenic forbidden clone(s) at the time of infection. Large-scale and rapid *fluctuations* of rates characteristic of infectious diseases are not seen where the major non-infectious fatal diseases are concerned. Recorded rates of lung cancer have admittedly shown a spectacular—though steady—increase in the course of this century (Burch, 1972, 1973), but the internal evidence of the rates themselves,

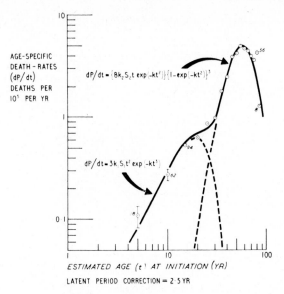

FIG. 10. As for Fig. 9. Data for Japan, 1960–63 (Segi and Kurihara, 1966). The parameters of the curves are: $k_1 = 9.4 \times 10^{-5}\text{yr}^{-3}$, $S_1 = 1.16 \times 10^{-4}$: $k_2 = 4.9 \times 10^{-4}\text{yr}^{-2}$, $S_2 = 2.2 \times 10^{-3}$.

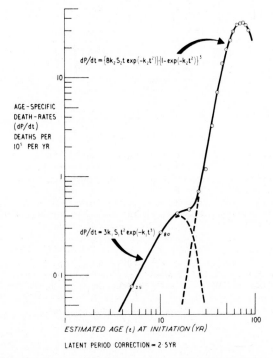

FIG. 11. As for Fig. 10. Data for US White women, 1960–63 (Segi and Kurihara 1966). The parameters of the curve are $k_1 = 1.71 \times 10^{-4}\text{yr}^{-3}$, $S_1 = 6.0 \times 10^{-5}$; $k_2 = 3.2 \times 10^{-4}\text{yr}^{-2}$, $S_2 = 2.0 \times 10^{-2}$.

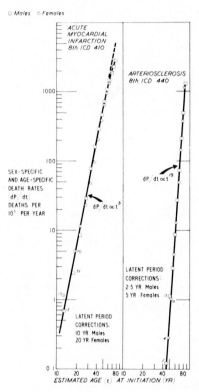

Fig. 12. Under certain conditions, dP/dt remains proportional to a constant power of t at all t of interest. Provided the usual requirements of the model are satisfied, this simple relation will be observed if the factor kt^r stays appreciably less than unity at all t of interest (Burch, 1966, 1968). For fatal diseases, this relation will also hold when all the following conditions, as well as the usual ones, are satisfied: (i) $n = 1$; (ii) $S = 1$; and (iii) the latent period between initiation and death is short. For acute myocardial infarction, England and Wales, 1970, age-specific death-rates corrected for latent period (10 yr males, 20 yr females) depart slightly from dP/dt proportional to t^5 above $t = 50$ yr, but fail to exhibit a mode (left hand panel). For arteriosclerosis, dP/dt remains proportional to t^{15} up to the highest age groups. With no defined mode, or curvature, values of k and S cannot be calculated. Numbers of deaths in 1970 from acute myocardial infarction were 60,363 males and 36,941 females; and from arteriosclerosis, 4,134 males and 7,044 females (Registrar General, 1972). Deaths in 1970 from all causes were: 292,053 male and 282,141 female.

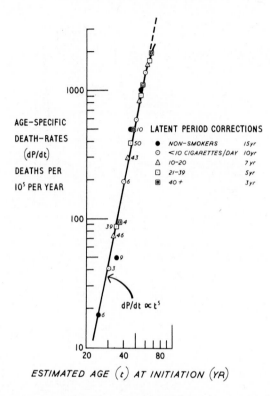

FIG. 13. Age-specific death-rates from "coronary heart disease" (roughly equivalent to "acute myocardial infarction" in Fig. 12), in relation to smoking habits of US male veterans (Kahn, 1966). Latent period corrections have been made to bring points on to the same initiation curve. The high rates of coronary heart disease at high levels of smoking can be interpreted in terms of a short latent period between initiation and death. Latent period is inversely related to the rate of cigarette smoking.

and autopsy findings over long periods, suggest that the recorded increase is largely or wholly an artefact arising from errors of diagnosis (Rosenblatt, 1969; Burch, 1973). Of course, a steady rate from year to year does not exclude an essential precipitating action by extrinsic factors such as microorganisms, allergens and stress. However, if such factors are essential they differ from those associated with the classical infectious diseases by being ubiquitous and of a non-epidemic character.

Suppose that extrinsic factors have only a modulating influence on the course of fatal conditions such as myocardial infarction and malignant diseases; we then need to consider whether it is possible to interfere effectively with the endogenous mechanisms of fatal diseases.

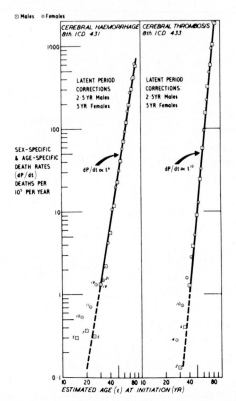

Fig. 14. Sex-specific and age-specific death-rates from cerebral haemorrhage (left panel) and cerebral thrombosis (right panel), England and Wales, 1970 (Registrar General, 1972). For both diseases, latent period corrections are 2·5 yr for males and 5 yr for females. Numbers of deaths were as follows: from cerebral haemorrhage, 7,377 male and 10,848 female; from cerebral thrombosis, 11,721 male and 18,683 female.

Extending the Life Span: Some Problems

In this section I assume that the general theory of disease outlined above is substantially correct. I consider, phase by phase, the more obvious problems that confront attempts to extend the life span of man.

GENOTYPE

It is widely recognized that the best recipe for a long life is the careful selection of parents. The scope for this recipe remains limited. For a few diseases with a simple pattern of inheritance, such as Huntington's chorea and familial intestinal polyposis, the early identification of gene carriers, combined with effective genetic counselling, could lead to a reduction of their already low frequency. The impact on the mean life span for the general population would be negligible. Unfortunately, for several of the major fatal diseases of old age it seems likely that all, or a large proportion, of the population is at genetic risk, although not necessarily at uniform risk. In such instances, there is little or no scope for changing genotypic frequencies through selective breeding, even if that were politically and socially feasible. The data of Figs. 12 and 14, showing the remorseless and steep dependence of death-rates on age, suggest that an optimum breeding programme would, at the best, achieve only small gains in average longevity. If, for example, all cancers were eradicated, diseases of the circulatory system would claim still more victims.

INITIATION PHASE

We have inferred that the somatic mutational events that initiate autoaggressive disease have many unfamiliar properties (Burch and Burwell, 1965; Burch, 1968). We have argued that probably they entail "DNA strand-switching". That is to say, in the mutational process the transcription of a gene in a growth-control stem cell switches spontaneously from the "normal" informational strand over to the complementary, anti-parallel strand. If, as we believe, strand-switching requires the spontaneous dissociation of a polypeptide chain from the (normally) non-informational strand of DNA, it is difficult to envisage how the rate of such events could be slowed under physiological conditions. Lowering the temperature of the cells at risk would be effective—and in fishes it is (Liu and Walford, 1966)—but in man, maintained hypothermia would appear to be incompatible with normal life. In view of the immense number of cells at risk, and the formidable difficulty of interfering with particular processes in the nucleus, the prospects of slowing the rate of somatic mutation through artificial intervention must be regarded as slender.

DEVELOPMENT PHASE

"Development" includes those multiple processes that occur subsequent to the completion of initiation. This phase of autoaggressive disease has been the most vulnerable to therapeutic and prophylactic intervention. The campaigns against infectious diseases have given medicine its most resounding victories. Through public health, immunization and antibiotics, the opportunities for microorganisms to invade the host and to monopolize his defence have been greatly curbed or even eliminated. Although battles remain to be won, the unconquered territory shrinks rapidly.

In certain non-infectious diseases (such as diabetes mellitus), metabolic imbalances can sometimes be rectified through substitutive (for example, insulin) therapy. Gains have also been achieved in connexion with malignant diseases. Surgical techniques improve. Aggressive chemotherapy has greatly lengthened survival from early-onset leukaemias and Burkitt's lymphoma: chemotherapy combined with radiotherapy has improved prognosis in Hodgkins' disease. But overall, the gains in the treatment of malignant diseases have been modest. As yet, no obvious paths to dramatic cures can be traced: the same holds true for circulatory diseases.

According to our theory, the elimination of non-infectious malignant and degenerative diseases would call for (i) the suppression or destruction of pathogenic forbidden clones; or (ii) the blocking, for example by immunological means, of the attack of forbidden clones of cells, or their humoral products, on target cells; or (iii) the repair, replacement or restoration of damaged target tissues, or correction of their malfunctioning. Some of the possibilities under (iii) have been and are being successfully exploited it is by no means certain that (i) and (ii) lie within the realms of the practicable. If autoaggressive disease results from a breakdown in the system of growth-control, therapeutic intervention needs to be highly specific if the general integrity of the organism is to be maintained.

Conclusions

Some scope remains for extending and refining "traditional" therapeutic and prophylactic methods: there is little reason to doubt that the slight downward trend of age-specific death-rates in the highest age-groups (Fig. 1c) will continue, at least for some years. However, we have no indications as yet that traditional methods will appreciably reduce mortality from the major malignant and degenerative diseases of the elderly. Neither have we sound reasons for hoping that changes of diet, the abolition of cigarettes, the outlawing of alcohol, the elimination of atmospheric pollution—and all the other canvassed nostrums—will bring about eternal life, or even a significant extension of life span.

The conquest of cancer, myocardial infarction and cerebrothrombosis may well call for measures not yet dreamed of. Diseases of this kind appear to me to result from intrinsic biological events and to be largely independent of extrinsic, controllable agents. When we have thoroughly explored the biological basis of disease we might be in a better position to outwit nature. But I see no reason to suppose that our final victory is assured.

References

Berkson, J. (1955). The statistical study of association between smoking and lung cancer. *Proc. Staff Meetings Mayo Clinic.* **35,** 367–385.

Burch, P. R. J. (1966). Spontaneous auto-immunity: equations for age-specific prevalence and initiation rates. *J. Theor. Biol.* **12,** 397–409.

Burch, P. R. J. (1968). *An Inquiry Concerning Growth, Disease and Ageing.* Edinburgh: Oliver and Boyd.

Burch, P. R. J. (1970). New approach to cancer. *Nature.* **225,** 512–516.

Burch, P. R. J. (1972). Smoking and health. *Lancet,* **i,** 1283; **ii,** 132–133, 1029, 1423–1424.

Burch, P. R. J. (1973). Smoking and cancer. *Lancet,* **i,** 939–940, 1315–1316; **ii,** 102–103.

Burch, P. R. J. and Burwell, R. G. (1965). Self and not-self: a clonal induction approach to immunology. *Q. Rev. Biol.* **40,** 252–279.

Burch, P. R. J. and Rowell, N. R. (1970). Lupus erythematosus. Analysis of the sex- and age-distributions of the discoid and systemic forms of disease in different countries. *Acta derm.-vener. Stockh.* **50,** 293–301.

Burch, P. R. J., Murray, J. J. and Jackson, D. (1971). The age-prevalence of arcus senilis, greying of hair and baldness. Etiologic considerations. *J. Geront.* **26,** 364–372.

Burnet, F. M. (1959). *The Clonal Selection Theory of Acquired Immunity.* London: Cambridge University Press.

Burnet, F. M. (1965). Somatic mutation and chronic disease. *Br. med. J.* **i,** 338–342.

Burnet, F. M. (1970). *Immunological Surveillance.* London: Pergamon Press.

Burwell, R. G. (1963). The role of lymphoid tissue in morphostasis. *Lancet,* **ii,** 69–74.

Cederlöf, R., Friberg, L. and Hrubec, Z. (1969). Cardiovascular and respiratory symptoms in relation to tobacco smoking: a study on American twins. *Archs envir. Hlth.* **18,** 934–940.

Choi, N. W., Schuman, L. M. and Gullen, W. H. (1970). Epidemiology of primary central nervous system neoplasms II case-control study. *Am. J. Epidemiol.* **91,** 467–485.

Doll, R., Payne, P. and Waterhouse, J. (1966). *Cancer Incidence in Five Continents.* International Union Against Cancer. Berlin: Springer-Verlag.

Doll, R., Muir, C. and Waterhouse, J. (1970). *Cancer Incidence in Five Continents.* Vol. II. (1970). International Union Against Cancer. Berlin: Springer-Verlag.

Eysenck, H. J. (1965). *Smoking, Health and Personality.* London: Weidenfeld and Nicolson.

Fisher, R. A. (1959). *Smoking. The Cancer Controversy.* Edinburgh: Oliver and Boyd.

Friberg, L., Cederlöf, R., Lorich, U., Lundman, T. and de Faire, U. (1973). Mortality in twins in relation to smoking habits and alcohol problems. A study on the Swedish Twin Registry. *Archs. envir. Hlth.* **27,** 294–304.

Jackson, D., Fairpo, C. G. and Burch, P. R. J. (1973). Distribution of symmetric and asymmetric patterns of caries attack in human permanent maxillary incisor teeth: genetic implications. *Archs. oral Biol.* **18,** 189–195.

Kahn, H. A. (1966). The Dorn study of smoking and mortality among U.S.

veterans. Report on 8½ years of observation. *National Institute Monograph.* No. 19. 1–125.

Liu, R. K. and Walford, R. L. (1966). Increased growth and life-span with lowered ambient temperature in the annual fish, *Cynolebias adloffi. Nature*, **212**, 1277–1278.

Registrar General. (1972). *Statistical Review of England and Wales for the Year 1970. Parts I and II.* London: Her Majesty's Stationery Office.

Rosenblatt, M. B. (1969). The increase in lung cancer; epidemic or artefact? *Medical Counterpoint.* **1**, 29–39.

Royal College of Physicians. (1971). *Smoking and Health Now.* London: Pitman Medical and Scientific Publishing Co. Ltd.

Segi, M. and Kurihara, M. (1966). *Cancer Mortality for Selected Sites in 24 Countries. No. 4. (1962–1963).* Japan: Sendai.

Seltzer, C. C. (1972a). Critical appraisal of the Royal College of Physicians' report on smoking and health. *Lancet.* **i,** 243–248.

Seltzer, C. C. (1972b). Smoking and health: *Lancet,* **i,** 586–588.

Seltzer, C. C. (1973). Cigarette smoking and longevity in the elderly. *Medical Counterpoint.* (In press).

Stell, P. M. (1972). Smoking and laryngeal cancer. *Lancet,* **ii,** 617–619.

Thomas, C. B. (1968). On cigarette smoking, coronary heart disease, and the genetic hypothesis, *Johns Hopkins Med. Jnl.* **122,** 69–76.

Thomas, C. B., Fargo, R. and Enslein, K. (1970). Personality characteristics of medical students as reflected by the strong vocational interest test with special reference to smoking habits. *Johns Hopkins Med. Jnl.,* **127,** 323–335.

Todd, G. F. (1972). *Statistics of Smoking in the United Kingdom.* Sixth edition. London: Tobacco Research Council.

Yerushalmy, J. (1971). The relationship of parent's cigarette smoking to outcome of pregnancy. Implications as to the problem of inferring causation from observed associations. *Am. J. Epidemiol.* **93,** 443–456.

The Future of Oral Contraception

CLIVE WOOD

Linacre College, Oxford, England

It is either a very brave man or a very foolish one who would speculate with any hope of certainty about the future of oral contraceptives. There could have been few people in 1956 when the first field trial of an oral contraceptive was initiated (Searle, 1964) who would have been able to predict that fifteen years later 20 million women throughout the world would be taking the pill (Speidal *et al.*, 1972) and that doctors and family planners almost without exception would agree that it represented by far the most effective form of reversible contraceptive that we had ever seen.

If the game of prediction was difficult then in the pioneering days, it has certainly become no easier now. The number of pill formulations has greatly increased. At the last count there were over twenty brands on the British market alone, and that was before the launch of a number of gestagen-only mini-pills at the end of last year. Several quite different approaches are currently being taken to the use of hormones (even oral hormones) for the prevention of pregnancy and it is not at all clear how much promise these differing approaches hold. The future then is murky. Nonetheless, I think that there are a few landmarks that we can see that allow us to speculate, if only in general terms, about the future and, either bravely or foolishly, I should like to try.

I will confess at the outset that the future that I predict is of the most conservative nature. I will suggest that none of the "new" approaches to hormonal contraception offer a promise of anything like the breakthrough that the original combined pill offered in terms of population control. I will suggest that from the point of view of major technical breakthroughs we are in a fairly stable situation and I would like to consider some of the reasons why this is so. I would also suggest that, for family planning on a large scale, sheer technical innovation is not perhaps the most important factor on which we should concentrate.

Problems of distribution of already existing formulations and problems of motivation in persuading women to use them and to persist in using them are at least as important to my mind as the problems that chemists and physiologists may currently be setting themselves in trying to devise new molecules, or new delivery systems.

The cornerstone of all our thinking about oral contraceptives is the combined contraceptive pill—a combination of an oestrogen together with one of many different types of progestagens. The hormones concerned are largely synthetic. They work together to produce controlled infertility and the hormone combinations that we now have are largely the result of trial and error over the last fifteen years.

We can perhaps start by considering one of the most important trends that oral contraceptives have undergone during that time. It is the trend from high dosage to low. Some of the first combined pills contained as much as 10 milligrams of a progestagen with up to 150 micrograms of an oestrogen. The latest of the new generation of low-dose pills contains half a milligram of a progestagen combined with only 30 micrograms of an oestrogen, a reduction in dosage of twenty times and five times respectively. I am well aware that different hormones differ in their potency—in their degrees of "oestrogenicity" or "gestagenicity" and that it is not strictly valid simply to compare numbers like this, but the trend to reduce dosage is a very real one, and with the right hormones in the right balance the effectiveness of the new tablet is just as great as that of the old ones, a result which was conclusively shown recently by, for example, Bye and Elstein (1973).

The trend to lower oestrogen dosage, in Britain at least, was, of course, largely the result of a statement made by the Committee for the Safety of Drugs in December 1969. The results of this statement were far-reaching, although Badaracco (1973) and others have shown that they were not entirely for the good. I cannot deal with them here, but I would commend anyone interested in the misinterpretation of medical information on a massive scale to review these papers.

The findings, for example of Inman and his co-workers (1970), on the correlation between the risk of thromboses of various types and the oestrogen content of the combined pill, acted as a spur not only for the reduction of the oestrogen content but also for the further development of pills containing no oestrogen at all. But it would be wrong to imagine that the much publicized "oestrogen scare" was entirely responsible for this development. The so-called "dawn of a new era" in oral contraception was said to be ushered in as early as September 1968 (Christie and Moore-Robinson, 1969) and trials on a number of different gestagen-only preparations were being conducted well before that time (see for example, Foss *et al.*, 1968). A number of new ones came on to the market at the end of 1972, and despite problems that have occurred with the alleged toxicity of some of the hormones concerned, the era of gestagen-only contraceptives is certainly here.

Anyone expecting dramatic advances in oral contraception will automatically ask whether mini-pills are "the answer"—the second generation contraceptive and the springboard for the future. And the reply appears to be "no". Although they are valuable for some women, gestagens alone without oestrogen have higher failure rates than the combined pill. In addition, some of them produce irregularities in the menstrual pattern that some women find intolerable. This indeed was the conclusion reached by Vessey and his co-workers (1972) after testing four different progestagen-only formulations. They wrote that "The results of this trial makes it seem unlikely that any currently available progestagen will be found to be capable of preventing conception without interfering with the menstrual cycle". Let me make it clear that I am not dismissing these gestagen-only mini-pills. Some synthetic hormones are clearly superior to others in this context, but I am suggesting that the contribution which any of them is likely to make to the overall future of hormonal contraception will be limited (see Ekstein *et al.*, 1972).

From the low-dose pill-a-day we ought perhaps to consider the pill-a-month or the three to six-monthly injection of contraceptive materials. Obviously, an effective and trouble-free, long-acting contraceptive would have many advantages, the principal one being its ability to overcome (to some extent at least) problems of distribution and, once the patient was initially "sold" on the idea, motivation too. But reactions to the use of such methods have been mixed. Leguia (1973), for example, has recently described his experiences with a combination of quinestrol and quingestanol acetate as a one-a-month oral contraceptive. His reported failure rate (3·8 pregnancies per 100 woman years) is the sort of figure that one would more usually associate with an intrauterine device than a contraceptive pill, and although he claims that control of the menstrual cycle is good, his report shows marked alterations of menstrual patterns, in some women at least.

Even more controversial are the results obtained with long-acting hormonal injections. These have been reviewed several times, (for example, IPPF, 1968; and Schwallie and Assenzo, 1973) and in some cases they have shown considerable promise. Very favourable pregnancy rates (in the order of 0·2 to 0·4 pregnancies per 100 women years) have been reported, and although the total disruption of any semblance of a menstrual cycle is often found, some women are happy to persist with the method which only has to be applied to them once every sixty or ninety days. Again, however, I do not think that anyone would pretend that long-acting oral or injectible contraceptives, at least in their present form, are going to supplant the "traditional" daily combined pill in the foreseeable future.

The subject of post-coital contraceptives has recently received a good deal of publicity (Blye, 1973) especially in the United States where the taking of diethyl stilboestrol (DES) amongst university students is said to have reached epidemic proportions. It is certainly true that high doses of certain oestrogens taken for five days, starting ideally within twenty-four hours of intercourse, will give a high degree of protection against pregnancy. The Food and Drug Administration in the United States has ruled that despite the dangers that might be associated with taking it, DES can legally be used in an emergency as a "morning-after" contraceptive (*Scrip*, 1973). However, they warn that it should not be considered as a "routine" contraceptive method and certainly the unpleasant (as opposed to hazardous) side effects of ingesting these quantities of oestrogen will mean that many girls and women find themselves in complete agreement. I understand that post-coital progestagens are also under study, but results are not so far available. In any event, I do not think that any post-coital treatment with whatever substance is likely to supplant the daily routine regimen that current pills provide.

Although my brief here is to discuss oral contraceptives I have already generalized it to some extent in considering injectibles. To generalize a little further, it is, I think, worth mentioning that other routes of administration of contraceptive hormones are being tried. Mishell and his co-workers (1970) considered the use of a vaginal ring and Scommegna and others (1970) of a device which would give a slow release of a gestagen directly into the uterine cavity. This type of approach allows the direct application of contraceptive hormones to the site at which they will be active. It opens the possibility of using dose levels which are potentially far less than those required for oral administration, and it also allows for the prolonged local action of the hormone for periods of, say, up to a year, following a single application. In a sense this approach combines the low-dose philosophy of current pills with the long-acting aspect of injectibles. Time alone will tell whether the current trials of such a device show this philosophy to be a practical one.

To return to the pill itself, I have suggested that the pill of the 'seventies is a low-dose combination, low particularly in oestrogen. I have indicated areas in which further "improvements" are being tried (in either eliminating the oestrogen altogether or producing a long-acting formulation) and I have suggested that in general these improvements represent only marginal advantages, applicable to some women but by no means representing an overall or revolutionary trend for the future.

But where will the revolutionary breakthrough in oral contraceptives come from? I confess that I do not know. Indeed I doubt whether another major breakthrough, as much a revolutionary improvement on the present pill as that pill itself was when it first appeared, is scheduled for the next ten years. I say this for a number of reasons, one of the strongest of which is not scientific at all, but commercial. Is there a pharmaceutical house in the world that can afford to develop a spectacular new breakthrough, assuming of course that it does not already have it in the pipeline, but rather that it is an untried molecule on the bench of the chemist who has just synthesised it? Health registration authorities doubtless act in our best interests in closely regulating the pharmaceutical products which can be put on to the market. But it has been estimated that the time necessary to develop a totally new contraceptive idea, to the stage where it would be allowed by the American Food and Drug Administration to come on to the market, may be as long as seventeen years, at a cost running into millions of dollars. The chances of recouping a reasonable return on this investment, at a time when patent lives are comparatively short and press comment about the hazards of the pill is still generally hostile, are by no means certain. An area of pharmaceutical research which looked extremely attractive a decade or so ago may well by now have lost much of its lustre to the only research organization currently capable of carrying out such research and development (see Christie, 1972).

If as seems likely to me at least, the future of oral contraceptives does not lie in spectacular innovations, does it follow that the pill has no future at all? Far from it. Oral contraceptives are still at the beginning rather than at the end of their useful lives as agents for population control. If we agree that we have today a whole range of (admittedly imperfect but extremely effective) formulations for the prevention of pregnancy, it could be argued that much of the effort that we spend in trying to bring about marginal or even major improvements in the technology should be spent instead in trying to boost the number of users of the current pill, both in developed and in developing nations. In the latter countries, of course, there are vast problems of motivation and distribution to be solved. But many of the lessons we can learn there are applicable here also, and *vice versa*.

I should mention the quite remarkable success that has been achieved in controlling the birth rate and improving both maternal and perinatal health in Aberdeen (Birth Control Campaign, 1973). This has been due in great measure to the provision of a realistic proportion of the Local Authority budget on a free family planning service. I do not wish to become involved here in the pros and cons of the free-contraceptive debate. But I introduce the point to show that *provision* as much as innovation can pay handsome dividends in the field of family planning. And this is particularly true of a method like the pill which already, and without further improvements, offers virtually 100 per cent protection from pregnancy to those women who are prepared to take it.

The great drawback of course to its more widespread provision is the fact that it requires a doctor's prescription. The hazards of the pill are constantly being reviewed (see for example Connell, 1972; Warren, 1973) and the excess risks of mortality and morbidity undergone by women on the pill are now fairly well documented. But so too are the hazards associated with an unwanted pregnancy, both in the Western world where they are comparatively small, and in the Third World where they are very much greater. In either of these hemispheres it has been shown by Potts (1968) and others that the risks of pregnancy greatly outweigh the risks of pill taking. Pill hazards can also be compared to the risks that we take every day for pleasure. Indeed, if one agrees with Potts that the hazards associated with the pill are "probably equivalent to smoking one third of one cigarette per day for three weeks out of four" then it is difficult to avoid his conclusion that "it would be more justifiable to have oral contraceptives in slot machines and restrict the sale of cigarettes to a medical prescription".

This latter argument is of course criticised by those who see pill taking as an *excess* risk over and above those risks of everyday life, but arithmetic of this sort gives strong emphasis to the notion that the provision of oral contraceptives by trained paramedical workers rather than solely by doctors (of whom there are simply not enough to go round) is the only way to obtain the full benefit of their potential in any family planning programme.

Fortunately, this attitude is slowly coming to be recognized. In the middle of 1970 the Central Medical Committee of the IPPF (IPPF, 1970) considered this question and concluded that "The Committee recognizes that the availability of medical personnel differs widely in different parts of the world. In areas where there is a shortage of doctors the distribution of steroidal contraceptives by paramedical personnel under medical supervision may free the physician's services for more demanding and urgent tasks."

The idea is also gaining ground in the United Kingdom, where there have been reports in the medical press that members of the Family Planning Association are considering the launch of a training scheme to equip lay workers (probably with nursing training) to carry out just such tasks under medical supervision. Detailed reasons why such an approach *must* be adopted, and a suggested format for the questionnaire that the nurse will use to screen out "high risk" patients from the pill-taking group, have been very clearly given by Speidal and his associates (1972).

In summary, I believe that oral contraceptives have a very significant future as a means both of large scale population control and, at the more domestic level, of child spacing and family planning. Such a statement is so obvious that I would apologise for making it were it not for the fact that I believe that the real future of oral contraceptives differs somewhat from that which is often, rather optimistically, imagined. Its immediate future lies, I think, not so much in the development of new hormonal preparations as in the utilization of those that we already have but whose full potential we have not even begun to exploit. I am certainly not advocating that hormonal research should cease, but I am seriously suggesting that we devote far more energy than at present to the problem of translating these research results, results that we already have, into practical birth-control policies.

References

Badaracco, M., Vessey, M. P. and Wiggins, P. (1973). Effect of the statement by the Committee on Safety of Drugs concerning oral contraceptives containing oestrogens on the contraceptive practices of women attending two family planning clinics. *J. Obstet. Gynaec. Brit. Cwlth.*, **80**, 355.

Birth Control Campaign (1973). *The Benefits of Birth Control.* London: Birth Control Campaign.

Blye, R. P. (1973). The use of oestrogens as post-coital contraceptive agents. *Am. J. Obstet. Gynec.*, **116**, 1044.

Bye, P. G. T. and Elstein, M (1973). Clinical assessment of a low-oestrogen combined oral contraceptive. *Br. med. J.*, **2**, 389.

Christie, G. A. (1972). Rate limiting factors in the development of new contraceptive methods. In *New Concepts in Contraception.* Edited by M. Potts and C. Wood. Oxford and Lancaster: Medical and Technical Publishing Co. Ltd.

Christie, G. A. and Moore-Robinson, M. (Editors) (1969). *Chlormadinone Acetate: A new Departure in Oral Contraception.* Maidenhead: Syntex Pharmaceuticals Ltd.

Connell, E. (1972). Current safety and status of the oral contraceptives. *Adv. Planned Parenthood*, **8**, 144. Excerpta Medica Conference Series no. 271.

Ekstein, P. Whitby, M., Fotherby, K., Butler, C., Mukherjee, T. K., Burnett, J. P. C., Richards, D. J. and Whitehead, T. P. (1972). Clinical and laboratory findings in a trial of Norgestrel, a low-dose progestagen-only contraceptive. *Br. med. J.*, **3**, 195.

Foss, G. L., Svendsen, E. K., Fotherby, K. and Richards, D. J. (1968). Contraceptive action of continuous low doses of Norgestrel. *Br. med. J.*, **2**, 489.

Inman, W. H. W., Vessey, M. P., Westerholm, B. and Engelund, A. (1970). Thromboembolic disease and the steroidal content of oral contraceptives. A report to the Committee on Safety of Drugs. *Br. med. J.*, **2**, 203.

I.P.P.F. (1968). Hormonal contraception. *International Planned Parenthood Medical Bulletin:* **2**, (3), 1.

I.P.P.F. (1970). Use of steroidal contraception justified. *International Planned Parenthood Federation Medical Bulletin:* **4** (2), 1.

Leguia, L. (1973). A Latin-American field trial with a once-a-month oral contraceptive. *J. reprod. Med.*, **10**, 202.

Mishell, D. R., Talas, M., Parlow, A. F. and Moyer, D. L. (1970). Contraception by means of a silastic vaginal ring impregnated with medroxyprogesterone acetate. *Am. J. Obstet. Gynec.*, **107**, 100.

Potts, M. (1968). Thromboembolism and the pill—new data. *International Planned Parenthood Federation Medical Bulletin:* **2** (4), 1.

Schwallie, P. C. and Assenzo, R. J. (1973). Contraceptive use-efficacy study utilizing medroxyprogesterone acetate administered as an intramuscular injection once every 90 days. *Fert. Steril*, **24**, 331.

Scommegna, A., Pandya, G. N., Christie, M., Lee, A. W. and Cohen, M. R. (1970). Intrauterine administration of progesterone by a slow releasing device. *Fert. Steril.*, **21**, 201.

Scrip. International Pharmaceutical News. (1973). DES as an emergency contraceptive. *Scrip*, **46**, 6.

Searle, G. D. & Co. 1964. *A prescription for family planning. The story of Enovid.* G. D. Searle, Reference and Resource Programme. New York.

Speidal, J. J., Ravenholt, R. T. and Perry, M. I. (1972). Non-clinical distribution of oral contraceptives. *Adv. Planned Parenthood.*, **8**, Excerpta Medical Conference Series 271, 28.

Vessey, M. P., Mears, E., Andolsek, L. and Ogrinc-Oven, M. (1972). Randomized double-blind trial of four progestagen-only contraceptives. *Lancet.*, **1**, 915.

Warren, M. P. (1973). Metabolic effects of contraceptive steroids. *Am. J. Med. Sci.*, **265**, 4.

New Technology for Voluntary Sterilization

M. J. FREE and G. W. DUNCAN

Battelle
Pacific Northwest Laboratories, Richland, Washington, U.S.A.
and
Population Study Center, Seattle, Washington, U.S.A.

The technologically-developed world has begun to see, feel, touch, smell and choke on the manifestations of over-consumption and over-population. The pioneer proponents of fertility control in the lesser developed countries are seeing their efforts outstripped by more easily practised and readily accepted death-control measures and impeded by cultural practices and religious dogma. Out of this growing awareness we see emerging the phenomenon of mass voluntary sterilization.

In the lesser-developed countries where the follow-up of individual patients is an impossible task and where repetitive procedures are easily forsaken or forgotten, the advantages of a contraceptive method requiring only one brief encounter between physician and individual to deliver nearly 100 per cent lifetime efficacy are overwhelming from a demographic and individual standpoint. Public health officials in some countries are realizing this and responding with vasectomy clinics in railway stations, country buses and camps. India has more than 19·3 sterilizations per 1,000 population (Pai, 1973). Eleven million sterilizations were recorded in that country by the end of May 1972. Only Bangladesh approached this rate of sterilization in the Eastern world although several other countries are on the way (Fig. 1).

In the Western world, and particularly in the USA, there is an increasing tendency for young people to accept sterilization as an irreversible commitment to limiting their families (Bumpass and Presser, 1972) and, apparently, as a way to get out from under the barrage of pills and paraphernalia (Presser and Bumpass, 1972a).

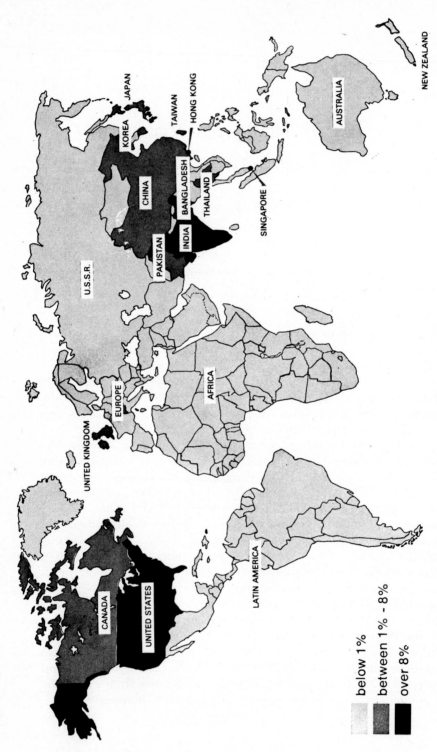

Fig. 1. Estimated world prevalence of voluntary sterilization 1972. Percentages are calculated on the basis of number of sterilized persons of reproductive age, male and female, per 100 women aged 15–44, in order to arrive at a figure indicating what percentage of fertile married couples are currently protected against unwanted pregnancy by this method. Source: Population Reports (1973).

below 1%

between 1% - 8%

over 8%

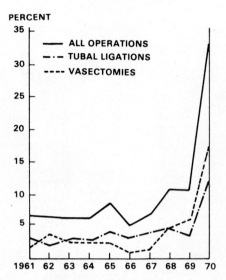

FIG. 2. Percentage of all sterile for contraceptive purposes in 1970 who were sterilized in each year: 1961–70. Source: Presser and Bumpass (1972b).

Figure 2 shows the trend in US vasectomies since 1961 (Presser and Bumpass, 1972b). One third of all people sterilized up to 1970 were sterilized in that year. Since that time the rate has doubled but is probably levelling off at the present time.

Male Sterilization

Male sterilization, or vasectomy, is a relatively simple doctor's office procedure (Fig. 3) salvaged from the arsenal of urological prophylactic procedures. It was formerly used to prevent the spread of urinary infection and made somewhat obsolete by antibiotics. In the 1920s, vasectomy was thought to increase sexual vigour (Steinach, 1920) and at the present time more than 13 million men are vasectomized throughout the world. Yet if vasectomy were a brand new procedure that had to be approved for human testing on the basis of animal experiments, it would have little chance of approval. The startling rise in popularity of the procedure, the dearth of organizable retrospective clinical information or controlled-perspective clinical studies and a spate of anecdotal clinical reports have stimulated a lot of laboratory activity in recent months. From these and earlier published studies we have learned of the spermatocoeles, adhesions and scrotal inflammation in rat (Smith, 1962; Flickinger, 1972; Alexander, 1973a; Sackler et al., 1973), the antibody-induced degeneration of germinal cells in guinea pig (Alexander, 1973b), the apparently pressure-

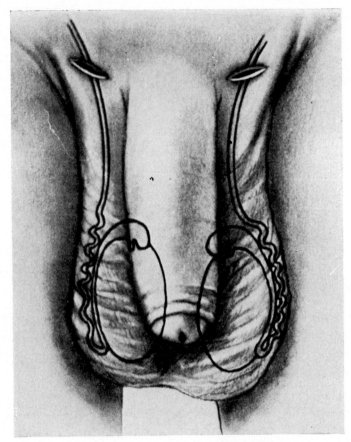

Fig. 3. Diagram showing optimum location for vasectomy. An outline of the testes, epididymides, and vasa deferentia is superimposed on the front view of the scrotum. Surgical incisions are shown over the straight portion of the vasa. Through these small incisions the vasa can be exteriorized and closed off by several alternative methods (see Fig. 6). Source: Schmidt (1972).

mediated necrosis of the testis in rabbit (Bedford, 1972), the epididymal and vasal granulomas in goat (unpublished data), all following occlusion of the vas deferens. All these changes are extensive and readily apparent to the trained observer and, to the degree that they occur in these animals, would not be tolerated in man.

Meanwhile, studies have been proceeding in a somewhat more dogged fashion on primates, including the human species itself. So far, while certainly revealing the room and need for improvement in traditional "cut and tie" methods of male sterilization, these studies are generally supporting the historical attitude of urologists who view vasectomy in man as a relatively innocuous procedure: as safe, certainly, as most alternative forms of pregnancy prevention and other everyday probabilities. For example, testosterone levels remained unchanged over a four-week study following vasectomy in fifty men (Bunge, 1972). Gonadotrophins and hematologic and blood-chemistry parameters remain unchanged over 0–12 months of a continuing study following vasectomy in ninety-five men (unpublished data). Of particular interest, serum uric acid and cholesterol remained unchanged over this time period. Normal spermatogenesis has been observed in testicular biopsies up to seventeen years after vasectomy (Johnson, 1972), although some transient changes may occur immediately following the operation (Derrick et al., 1973) and sperm granulomas occur in up to ten per cent of cases depending on the method of vas occlusion employed (Schmidt and Morris, 1973). Evidence that many reported effects in man are psychological is suggested by the unaltered sexual activity of Rhesus monkey following vasectomy (Phoenix, 1973). The one clear-cut change that does occur following vasectomy in a significant percentage of men is the build up of sperm antibody titers (Phadke and Padukone, 1966; Ansbacher et al., 1972; Shulman et al., 1972). This will be discussed later in the context of reversibility of vasectomy.

At least ten additional studies are presently being conducted in U.S. clinics and laboratories on vasectomized human volunteers or subhuman primates. Thus much more information on the sequelae of vasectomy in these key species will become available in the next one or two years and will hopefully make unnecessary any further extrapolation of experimental data from unsatisfactory animal models. One reason for the differences in response to vasectomy between man and lower mammals may well have to do with the innervation of the epididymis. The middle spermatic nerve courses safely along the spermatic artery in man, whereas in lower mammals its equivalent accompanies, and probably suffers the same fate as, the vas deferens.

There is now the debatable question that is causing some divergence in the objectives of medical scientists and clinicians working in this field: Would significantly more people accept vasectomy if it were a reversible procedure? In some of the lesser-developed countries, where the dependence on children for support in old age and concomitant fear of child mortality is a major factor for birth control acceptability (Pai, 1973), the answer to the question is most likely to be "yes". In the technologically developed countries, where the motives for voluntary sterilization may perhaps have a higher ideological or philosophical content, the answer to the question is less certain.

Within the ranks of those who view vasectomy as a reversible or potentially reversible procedure, there is another divergence of opinion. Firstly, there are those who view the reanastomosis of the vas deferens by surgical means as a practical and potentially generally applicable procedure and see a need for technological innovation only in the surgical tools for carrying out this procedure. These tools may include tissue adhesives (Bornemisza and Furka, 1970; Gursel *et al.*, 1971) or various types of splints (Steinhardt, 1969). On the other hand, there are those who believe that reversibility of vasectomy would be facilitated by the development of a valve-like device which could be implanted into the vas deferens in lieu of vasectomy and would allow sperm to stop or go at the will of the individual and the hand of the surgeon. Several laboratories and clinics are pursuing the idea of a reversible intravasal occlusive device (Table I). These devices range from the well publicized gold and stainless steel Bionyx "Phaser" currently being tested in human volunteers at New York Medical College (Fig. 4) to various plastic, ceramic and metal devices. Details of some of these devices including the gold Phaser are not public information at the present time. Our own model (Fig. 5), as an example of the plastic genre of devices, incorporates much of the current thinking on optimizing anatomic and physiologic conditions for reversal of vas occlusion. It is easily and cheaply fabricated, can be installed in the vas with a minimum of disturbance to blood, nerve, lymph and muscle continuity, will bind to the vas by allowing and promoting tissue ingrowth, is sufficiently compliant to respond to tissue deformation and muscular compression, will totally block the passage of sperm through the vas, is easily reversible by surgical intervention and permits verification of potency at the time of reversal. It is currently being tested in animals.

Common to both objectives, the intravasal device or surgical reanastomosis, is a need for improved methods of simple vasectomy that would facilitate restoration of fertility if that need arose in the individual. A large number of variations of the basic procedure of vasectomy are utilized on a routine basis around the world (Klapproth and Young, 1973). In the near future there will undoubtedly be some extensive comparative studies of these methods. There is now a growing awareness of the need to maintain nerve, blood vessel, lymphatic and even muscle continuity in the vas deferens if reversibility is to be optimized. It seems likely that the current practice of removing segments of varying lengths from the vas deferens will be found to be unnecessary providing the mucosal lining of the vas is interrupted and effectively prevented from regenerating.

TABLE I

Current or recent research in the U.S.A. on reversible intravasal devices

Institution (Principal investigators)	Funding agency	Concept
New York Medical College, School of Medicine (M. Freund and J. Davis)	NIH (NICHHD)	Gold and stainless steel stop-cock installed in the sectioned vas with gold mesh for in-growth.
Ortho Pharmaceutical Corporation, Baritan, New Jersey.	Ortho	Metal device with magnetic valve for nonsurgical reversal.
Illinois Institute of Technology Research Institute Chicago, Ill., (E. E. Brueschke)	NIH (NICHHD)	Porous ceramic and etched stainless steel operated through a small opening in scrotal sac or by palpating scrotum. I sections conduits used.
Abcor Inc. Cambridge, Mass. (E. W. Nuwayser)	NIH (NICHHD)	Hollow fibre tube with bonded flock. Centre pin made of steel, vitallium or plastic.
Tecna Corp. Emeryville, California.	NIH	Plastic tubes with micropor-ous surface for tissue ingrowth.
Illinois Institute of Technology Research Institute Chicago, Ill. (M. Burns and E. E. Brueschke)	AID (?)	Perivasal occlusive device—occludes by external com-pression.
University of Missouri Columbia, Mo. (E. C. Mather)	NIH (NICHHD)	Reversible vasectomy pros-thesis.
Medical Engineering Foundation Inc. Little Rock, Ark. (J. T. Turley)	?	Ball valve device made of fluoroplastic material. Flexible stems installed through a slit in the unsectioned vas by means of a special inverted V clamp. Valve kept in place by rolled plastic clip. Ball valve has slotted head.
Battelle Northwest Laboratories, Richland, Wash. (M. J. Free)	AID	Flexible plastic device with textured surface installed into the unsectioned vas in two halves. Halves are joined around a plastic plug and uncoupled and rejoined around open tube for reversal.

TABLE I (continued)

Institution (Principal investigators)	Funding agency	Concept
Southwest Foundation for Res. and Dev. San Antonio, Tex. (D. C. Kraemer)	NIH (NICHHD)	Nonocclusive device with copper or iron coils or threads inside a tube—spermicidal action.
Massachusetts General Hospital, Boston, Mass.	Population Council Inc.	Removable silastic obturator.
Carolina Population Center, U. North Carolina, Chapel Hill, N.C. (J. Hulka)	AID	Polypropylene tube with teflon velour. Also a proplast sponge.
Dept. of Urology Univ. of Iowa, Iowa City, Ia. (K. H. Moon and R. G. Bunge)	?	Tapered polyethylene tubing installed in unsectioned vas with ends protruding. Ends are anchored with silver clips.

The electrocautery is finding increasing acceptance in the United States as a tool for improving simple vasectomy. Schmidt recently reported a series of 1,000 vasectomies in which no segment of the vas was removed and no ligatures were tied on the vas (Fig. 6) (Schmidt, 1973). Rather, the lumen of the proximal end was cauterized for 4 mm in such a way that the lesion was confined to the epithelium, lamina propria and part of the muscle wall. The distal end was cauterized on the cut surface only and the sheath of the vas was closed over it with a single ligature. This series now stands at 1,500 with no failures and less than one per cent of sperm granulomas or other complications (Schmidt, S. S. personal communication). This compares with around 0·5–3 per cent failures and up to 10 per cent of complications following vasectomy by ligation (Fig. 6) (Klapproth and Young, 1973); Schmidt, 1973). An additional advantage is that reanastomosis is technically easier following vasectomy by this procedure.

A bipolar electrocautery specifically designed for vas occlusion has been developed in our laboratory under the sponsorship of AID (Fig. 7). This small solid-state instrument is completely self-contained and draws very little power from its $22\frac{1}{2}$ volt battery. The probe is sterilizable and the needle electrode interchangeable. Current flow is confined to the area between the two bands around the tip of the needle (Fig. 8) and is thus self-limiting. This device is currently under clinical evaluation and shows promise for improving simple vasectomies under field, railway station, bus or clinic conditions.

FIG. 4. The gold and stainless steel Bionyx "Phaser" device for reversible occlusion of the vas. See Table I.

Plans are also proceeding to adapt this device for a transcutaneous approach to vas occlusion. This approach would minimize surgical procedure and avoid visible scarring by cauterizing the lumen of the vas by inserting the electrode through the skin of the upper scrotum. No fascial barrier would be interposed in the sperm path using this method. However, our experience in animals suggests that the fibrous tissue ingrowth from lamina propria or muscle layers of the vas may constitute a sufficient barrier to sperm flow providing that discontinuity of the epithelial layer is assured. The failure and complication rate associated with cauterizing the intact (unsectioned) vas are unknown at the present time and anatomical variation may preclude use of such a procedure in some individuals.

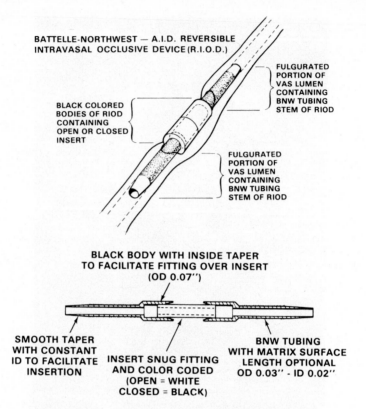

FIG. 5. The plastic "RIOD" device for reversible occlusion of the vas. See text for details. (Upper) Cross section. (Lower) The RIOD installed in the vas deferens.

An incisionless approach to vas occlusion has already been made by Sekhon in India using transcutaneous diathermy to transect the vas in one or two places (Sekhon, 1970). Other approaches to simple vas occlusion include the insertion of silicone plugs, thread and tubes that simply fill up the vas lumen (Lee, 1969; Klapproth and Young, 1973). It seems unlikely that these indwelling plugs will stand up to extensive testing without some form of adhesion or ingrowth with the wall of the vas. Tantalum clips are currently being used instead of ligatures in at least one clinic (Moss, 1972) and are being promoted for the purpose of vas and tubal occlusion by the manufacturer of hemoclips (Edward Weck and Co. Inc., New York). Looking further into the future, the use of injectable substances that induce scar tissue plugs in the vas remains a possibility. Amongst the latter studies, the recent report of Freeman and Coffey, (1973) using ethanol injection into the rat

Failures

Failures
and
spermatic
granuloma

I

3%

7·3%

1 cm Segment
┌─ **Excised** ─┐

II

0%

9·7%

**Fascial
Sheath
Sutured**

III

0%

1·0%

Fulguration

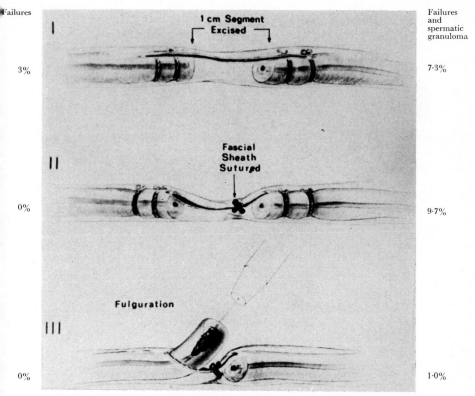

FIG. 6. Results of different methods of vasectomy. I, vas cut, doubly ligated and 1 cm segment excised. II, vas cut, doubly ligated, 1 cm segment excised and distal end covered over with fascial sheath. III, vas cut, proximal lumen fulgurated, distal end covered over with fascial sheath. Source: Schmidt (1973).

vas is of notable interest. In addition, quinacrine dihydrochloride has shown some vas occlusive effects in the rat vas (Setty *et al.*, 1972). The use of focused ultrasound for transcutaneous vasal cauterization has also been proposed by our laboratory and is in the preliminary design state at the present time.

Assuming that sperm can be returned to the ejaculate in sufficiently large numbers, will that achieve the objective of restored fertility? The currently available figures (Derrick, 1973) for surgical reanastomosis show a large discrepancy between success in restoring sperm levels and restoration of fertility (Table II). A more successful individual series yielded 55 per cent pregnancy with 83 per cent return of sperm in 76 patients (Phadke and Phadke, 1967). Indications are that these observations are linked with others showing an increase in

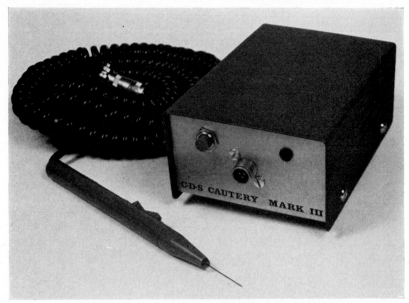

Fig. 7. A miniature, battery-powered bipolar cautery unit for use in the vas deferens.
Source: Decker and Carmichael (1973.)

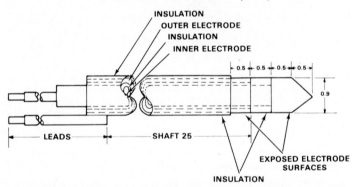

Fig. 8. Detail of the bipolar needle electrode for vas cautery unit. Source: Decker and
Carmichael (1973).

antibody titers in 50–60 per cent of men following vasectomy (Phadke
and Padukone, 1966; Ansbacher *et al.*, 1972; Shulman *et al.*, 1972). If
these antibodies are found to impair epididymal function or spermatogenesis it may well be that all methods of vasectomy reversal will
have only limited success unless some more sophisticated immunological precautions are taken. Additionally, the long-term pathological
consequences, if any, of autoimmunity to sperm are unknown and are
the subject of considerable research activity at the present time.

TABLE II
Survey of vasovasostomy

No. of physicians	Technique	No. of cases	% pregnancy
103	No splint	388	10·9
281	Wire splint	804	19·9
98	Cannulae splint	242	20·9
60	Nylon splint	196	26·0
542			19·3

Return of normal sperm in 38 %

Female Sterilization

Occlusion of the fallopian tubes in the human female presents many of the same ponderables as vas occlusion: to section or not to section; to remove a segment or not; to use clips or ligatures; to cauterize or not, to determine the optimum site of occlusion. In addition, female sterilization poses other sets of alternatives and attendant problems concerned with preoperative treatment, timing of the procedure and approach to the site of occlusion. Many of these alternatives are falling into line behind a few key technological innovations. The most profound of these innovations has been the development of fibre optics and the evolution of the endoscope to the status of an everyday surgical instrument. This instrument in the form of a laparoscope has turned female sterilization into an outpatient procedure in some clinics (Wheeless, 1972a, b; Wortman and Piotrow, 1973a), eliminating the risks associated with general anaesthesia, the expense associated with inpatient care, and the scar associated with the traditional laparotomy approach. Although most laparoscopists use general anaesthesia and two punctures to accommodate laparoscope and occlusioning tools (Neuwirth, 1972; Wortman and Piotrow, 1973a), the instrumentation and techniques have been developed for viewing and doing through a single abdominal puncture (Wortman and Piotrow, 1973b). Lower surgical risk, less scarring and greater acceptability of local anaesthesia are likely to make single puncture laparoscopy a major method in the future.

Another endoscopic technique, culdoscopy, approaches the occluding site through the vagina rather than abdomen (Fig. 9). It has all the advantages of laparoscopy. Additionally, it does not require insufflation of the abdominal cavity, leaves no external scarring and avoids the psychological trauma associated with abdominal surgery

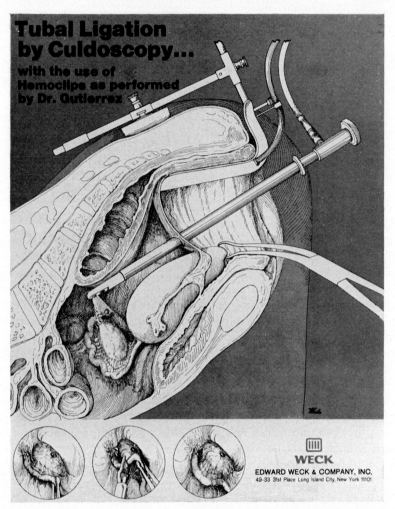

Fig. 9. Tubal Ligation by Culdoscopy. Source: Advertising brochure. Edward Weck and Company, Inc. 49–33 31st Place, Long Island City, New York 11101.

(Clyman, 1972; Gutierrez-Najar, 1972). However, it apparently requires more skill and therefore, more training and experience. Consequently, extensive future use of this method may be primarily centred around large clinics.

All of these endoscopy methods suffer from the disadvantage of instrument cost, higher for laparascopy because of the equipment needed to pump $CO_2(N_2O$ or, rarely, air) into the body cavity. Because of this and also because some endoscopic techniques are not suited to post-partum or post-abortion sterilization, it is unlikely that the traditional methods will die out completely. In particular, the non-endoscopic transcervical procedure, colpotomy, requires the minimum of surgical equipment, can be done under local anaesthesia and is probably adaptable to outpatient procedure, making it ideal for widespread application in developing countries (Wortman and Piotrow, 1973c).

Methods of actually occluding the fallopian tubes have included ligatures usually accompanied by sectioning, cautery with or without sectioning, tantalum hemoclips (Gutierrez-Najar, 1972; Hayashi, 1972) and more recently plastic and metal spring loaded clips which maintain constant tension on the tubes, thereby preventing necrosis and recanalization (Hulka and Omran, 1972a). Refinement of the surgical tools for applying these latter clips in conjunction with culdoscopy or colpotomy may significantly simplify the overall procedure and further increase its practicability and acceptability in the next few years.

For the longer term, it seems certain that non-surgical procedures of sterilization will become practical. These will utilize the transcervical approach and need, therefore, no more skill than that required to install an intrauterine contraceptive device. Use of the hysteroscope will allow direct visualization of the uterotubal junction if necessary. The methods of occlusion may be by chemical or inert liquids in the form of adhesives (Grode et al., 1971; Falb et al., 1972), barriers (Rakshit, 1968 and 1972; Omran and Hulka, 1970), sclerosing agents (Richarrt et al., 1971; Zipper and Insunza, 1972; Zipper et al., 1970) or combinations of these, or may involve electrocautery (Hulka and Omran, 1972b) or, more remotely, cryocoagulation (Droegemueller et al., 1971), laser beams (Halbrecht, in press) and ultrasonic cautery.

Quinacrine has proved to be the most effective chemical tubal occlusion agent to date (Zipper and Insunza, 1972), although it requires two applications to achieve effective tubal obstruction in 90 per cent of cases. Among the adhesive agents, gelatin-resorcinol-formaldehyde (GRF.) has shown promise (Grode et al., 1971).

Devices are being developed to deliver chemical occlusive agents precisely to the fallopian tubes without endoscopic visualization (Thompson et al., 1972). They would act to seek out the uterotubal junction and form a gasket around it to prevent the back flow of injected chemicals. The chemicals may then be injected into the tubes from an external syringe. Such devices are the key to making female sterilization a paramedical procedure, thereby increasing its availability in more remote and sparsely-doctored areas of developing countries or regions.

Summary of Future Trends

Although a temporary slowing of the current rate of voluntary vasectomy in the technologically-developed countries seems inevitable as the once-only demands of motivated individuals are satisfied and the procedure undergoes close scientific scrutiny, the demands for female sterilization may continue to grow unabated as procedures become simpler, safer, and cheaper. In the developing countries, delivery of the means rather than acceptability of family limitation is the limiting factor. While instrument costs and maintenance problems may hobble the increase of female sterilization procedures until transcervical methods become practical, it seems likely that female sterilization will play a steadily increasing rôle in the birth control programmes of the developing world. More reversible methods of vas occlusion, feasible within the next five years, should boost the acceptability of this procedure in a younger and therefore more demographically-significant segment of the developing world population.

References

Alexander, N. J. (1973a). Ultrastructural changes in rat epididymis after vasectomy. *Z. Zellforsch*, **136**, 177.

Alexander, N. J. (1973b). Vasectomy and autoimmune aspermatogenesis in the guinea pig. *6th Annual Meeting, Society for Study of Reproduction*, Athens, Georgia.

Ansbacher, R., Keung-Yeung, K. and Wurster, J. C. (1972). Sperm antibodies in vasectomised men. *Fertil. Steril.*, **23**, 640.

Bedford, J. M. (1972). The consequences of vasectomy for the vas deferens and epididymis in the rat, hamster, rabbit and rhesus monkey. Presented at *Annual Conference, Society for Study of Fertility*. Reading, England.

Bornemisza, G. and Furka, I. (1970). Restoration of the divided ductus deferens by adhesive material. *Acta Chir. Acad. Sci. Hung.*, **11**, 335.

Bumpass, L. L. and Presser, H. B. (1972). Contraceptive sterilization in the U.S.: 1965 and 1970. *Demography*, **9**, 531.

Bunge, R. G. (1972). Plasma testosterone levels in man before and after vasectomy. *Invest. Urol.*, **10**, 9.

Clyman, M. J. (1972). Tubal sterilization by operative culdoscopy. In *Female Sterilization*. Edited by G. W. Duncan, R. D. Falb and J. J. Speidel. New York: Academic Press.

Decker, J. and Carmichael, R. (1973). An elecrocautery instrument for the fulguration of the vas deferens during vasectomy for sterilization. (Presented at the Tenth Annual Rocky Mountain Bioengineering Symposium). Pittsburgh, Pennsylvania: Instrument Society of America.

Derrick, F. C. (1973). Survey on reanastomosis. Reported at *29th Annual Meeting, American Fertility Society*, San Francisco, and summarized in *Family Planning Digest*, **2**, 7.

Derrick, F. C., Glover, W. L., Kanjuburumbam, Z., and Jacobson, C. (1973). Histopathological changes in spermatogenesis following vas deferens occlusion. *29th Annual Meeting, American Fertility Society*, San Francisco.

Droegemueller, W., Makowski, E. and Macsalka, R. (1971). Destruction of the endometrium by cryosurgery. *Amer. J. Obstet. Gynecol.*, **110**, 467.

Falb, R. D., Grode, G. A. and Pavkov, K. L. (1972). Adhesive blockage of the fallopian tube. In *Female Sterilization*. Edited by G. W. Duncan, R. D. Falb and J. J. Speidel. New York: Academic Press.

Flickinger, C. J. (1972). Alterations in the fine structure of the rat epididymis after vasectomy. *Anat. Rec.*, **173**, 277.

Freeman, C. and Coffey, D. S. (1973). Chemical induction of male sterility by injection of vaso-sclerosing agents. *Fed. Proc.*, **32**, 310 Abs.

Grode, G. A., Pavkov, K. L. and Falb, R. D. (1971). Feasibility study on the use of a tissue adhesive for the nonsurgical blocking of fallopian tubes. Phase I: Evaluation of a tissue adhesive. *Fertil. Steril.*, **22**, 522.

Gursel, E., Zinsser, H. H. and Hrdlicka, G. (1971). Nonsutured, nonsplinted anastomosis of the vas deferens: A preliminary report. *Invest. Urol.*, **8**, 417.

Gutierrez-Najar, A. J. (1972). Culdoscopy as an aid to family planning. In *Female Sterilization*. Edited by G. W. Duncan, R. D. Falb and J. J. Speidel. New York: Academic Press.

Halbrecht, I. In Proceedings of the 2nd International Conference on Voluntary Sterilization, February 25–March 1, 1973, Geneva, Switzerland. *Excerpta Medica* (in press).

Hayashi, M. (1972). Tubal sterilization with clips. In *Human Sterilization*. Edited by R. M. Richart and D. J. Prager. Springfield, Illinois: C. C. Thomas Co.

Hulka, J. F. and Omran, K. F. (1972a). Comparative tubal occlusion: Rigid and spring-loaded clips. *Fertil. Steril.* **23**, 633.

Hulka, J. F. and Omran, K. F. (1972b). Cauterization for tubal sterilization. In *Human Sterilization*. Edited by R. M. Richart and D. J. Prager. Springfield, Illinois: C. C. Thomas Co.

Johnson, D. S. (1972). Reversible male sterilization: Current status and future directions. *Contraception*, **5**, 327.

Klapproth, H. J. and Young, I. S. (1973). Vasectomy, vas ligation and vas occlusion. *Urology*, **1**, 292.

Lee, H. Y. (1969). Experimental studies on reversible vas occlusion by intravasal thread. *Fertil. Steril.*, **20**, 735.

Moss, W. M. (1972). A sutureless technic for bilateral partial vasectomy. *Fertil. Steril.*, **23**, 33.

Neuwirth, R. S. (1972). Nonpuerperal sterilization by laparoscopy. In *Human Sterilization*. Edited by R. M. Richart and D. J. Prager. Springfield, Illinois: C. C. Thomas Co.

Omran, K. K. and Hulka, J. F. (1970). Tubal occlusion: A comparative study. *Int. J. Fertil.*, **15**, 226.

Pai, D. N. (1973). *Keynote Address of the 2nd Int. Conference of the Assoc. Volunt. Steri.* Geneva.

Phadke, A. M. and Padukone, K. (1966). Presence and significance of autoanti-bodies against spermatozoa in the blood of men with obstructed vas deferens. *J. Reprod. Fertil.*, **7**, 163.

Phadke, G. M. and Phadke, A. G. (1967). Experiences in the reanastomosis of the vas deferens. *J. Urol.*, **97**, 888.

Population Reports, Series C-D, (Feb. 1973). Population Information Program, Dept. of Medical and Public Affairs of the George Washington University, Medical Center, 2001 S St., N. W., Washington D.C. 20009, U.S.A.

Phoenix, C. H. (1973). Sexual behaviour in rhesus monkeys after vasectomy. *Science*, **179**, 493.

Presser, H. B. and Bumpass, L. L. (1972a). The acceptability of contraceptive sterilization among U.S. couples: 1970. *Family Planning Perspectives*, **4**, 18.

Presser, H. B., and Bumpass, L. L. (1972b). "Demographic and Social Aspects of Contraceptive Sterilization in the United States. 1965–70." Report to the Commission on Population Growth and the American Future, In *Demographic and Social Aspects of Population Growth.* Edited by C. F. Westoff and R. Parke, Jnr. U. S. Government Printing Office, Washington, D. C. February.

Rakshit, B. (1968). Experiments on tubal blocking for sterilization without laparotomy. *J. Obstet. Gynecol., India,* **18,** 282.

Rakshit, B. (1972). Scope of liquid plastics and other chemicals for blocking the fallopian tube. In *Human Sterilization.* Edited by R. M. Richart and D. J. Prager. Springfield, Illinois: C. C. Thomas Co.

Richarrt, R. M., Gutierrez-Najar, A. J. and Neuwirth, R. S. (1971). Transvaginal human sterilization: A preliminary report. *Amer. J. Obstet. Gynecol.,* **111,** 108.

Sackler, A. M., Weltman, A. S., Pandhi, V. and Schwartz, R. (1973). Gonadal effects of vasectomy and vasoligation. *Science,* **179,** 293.

Schmidt, S. S. (1972). Vas reanastomosis procedures, In *Human Sterilization.* Edited by R. M. Richarrt and D. J. Prager. Illinois: C. C. Thomas.

Schmidt, S. S. (1973). Prevention of failure in vasectomy. *J. Urtol.,* **109,** 296.

Schmidt, S. S. and Morris, R. R. (1973). Spermatic granuloma: The complication of vasectomy. *Fertil. Steril.* (In press).

Sekhon, G. S. (1970). Percutaneous vasectomy, a comparative study using a new instrument and technique. *Indian J. Med. Res.,* **58,** 1433.

Setty, B. S., Dasgupta, P. R. and Kar, A. B. (1972). Chemical occlusion of the vas in rats. *Contraception,* **6,** 329.

Shulman, S., Zappi, E., Ahmed, U. and Davis, J. E. (1972). Immunologic consequences of vasectomy. *Contraception,* **5,** 269.

Smith, G. (1962). The effects of ligation of the vasa efferentia and vasectomy on testicular function in the adult rat. *J. Endocrinol.,* **23,** 385.

Steinach, E. (1920). Verjuengung durch experimentelle neubelebung des altenden pubertaetsdruese. *Arch. Entwiklungsmech. Organismen,* **46,** 557.

Steinhardt, E. E. (1969). Vasovasostomy—a simplified technique. *Henry Ford Hosp. Med. J.,* **17,** 67.

Thompson, H., Dafoe, C. A., Moulding, T. S. and Seitz, L. E. (1972). Evaluation of experimental methods of occluding the utero tubal junction. In *Female Sterilization.* Edited by G. W. Duncan, R. D. Falb and J. J. Speidel. New York: Academic Press.

Wheeless, C. R. (1972)a. The status of outpatient tubal sterilization by laparoscopy: Improved techniques and review of 1,000 cases. *Obstet. Gynecol.,* **39,** 635.

Wheeless, C. R. (1972b). Outpatient sterilization by laparoscopy under local anaesthesia in less developed countries. In *Female Sterilization.* Edited by G. W. Duncan, R. D. Falb and J. J. Speidel. New York: Academic Press.

Wortman, J. and Piotrow, P. T. (1973a). Laparoscopic sterilization, a new technique. *Sterilization, Population Report,* Series C, No. 1, January.

Wortman, J. and Piotrow, P. T. (1973b). Laparoscopic sterilization II. What are the Problems? *Sterilization, Population Report,* Series C, No. 2, March.

Wortman, J. and Piotrow, P. T. (1973c). Colpotomy—the vaginal approach. *Sterilization, Population Report,* Series C, No. 3, June.

Zipper, J. and Insunza, S. (1972). Pharmacological agents that potentiate or inhibit the occlusive action of quinacrine in the rabbit tube and rat uterus. In *Female Sterilization.* Edited by G. W. Duncan, R. D. Falb and J. J. Speidel. New York: Academic Press.

Zipper, J., Stachetti, E. and Medel, M. (1970). Human fertility control by transvaginal application of quinacrine on the fallopian tube. *Fertil. Steril.,* **21,** 581.

Prostaglandin and Other Methods of Early Termination of Pregnancy

G. M. FILSHIE

Department of Obstetrics and Gynaecology, University of Nottingham, Nottingham, England

Termination of pregnancy is now a recognized method of dealing with unwanted and unplanned pregnancies. It is often referred to as "hindsight family planning", as it is only employed after the event of sexual intercourse. There are at present a whole range of methods for terminating pregnancy, and these are often related to the gestation of pregnancy. Before discussing in detail the early methods which are available, all the common methods should be enumerated to put the early methods into perspective. The spectrum of methods is shown in Fig. 1.

Immediately after unprotected intercourse, high-dose oestrogens have been given orally for 5 days. This does not appear to interfere with fertilization, but it does inhibit implantation. Up to 10 days late with a menstrual period, prostaglandins may be given to cause early abortion or to induce menstruation. Up to 21 days late with a period (or 7 weeks amenorrhoea), menstrual extraction may be performed using a 4 mm Karman curette. Between 6 weeks and 12 weeks amenorrhoea, the larger Karman curette may be used (6, 8, or 10 mm curette). Local anaesthesia is used and the procedure is done on an out-patient procedure. The Berkley cannula is used as an alternative in some centres. These last three methods represent early methods of termination of pregnancy, and these are discussed in more detail later.

From 6 weeks to 14 weeks amenorrhoea, a Bierer-type curette is often used in conjunction with general anaesthesia. This is an in-patient procedure. So too is the time-hallowed D and C, which although it is still practised by many, is rapidly being replaced by suction methods.

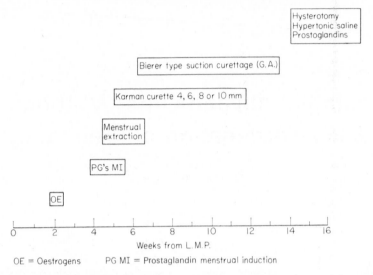

OE = Oestrogens   PG MI = Prostaglandin menstrual induction

Fig. 1. Methods of terminating pregnancy.

In the second trimester of pregnancy, a variety of methods are employed. Traditionally, hysterotomy was performed. This is now replaced by intra-amniotic instillation of hypertonic solutions including saline, glucose, urea or mannitol. Prostaglandins have been administered by various routes with favourable results. Methods such as the insertion of rubber catheters or "super coils" are not generally regarded as safe methods.

Induction of the Delayed Menstrual Period with Prostaglandins

The past five years have demonstrated a dramatic upsurge of interest inthe field of prostaglandins. Prostaglandins is the generic name for a number of chemically related compounds, which are smooth muscle stimulants and vasodepressor agents. They are 20 carbon-atom-hydroxy fatty acids, which have a cyclopentane ring. There are fourteen different naturally occurring prostaglandins which are present in many biological tissues in man, including the seminal vesicles, endometrium, lung, renal medulla, the thyroid gland, stomach, gut and salivary glands. Prostaglandins are known to be fundamentally involved in uterine contractility at all times. Exogenous prostaglandins were used clinically first to initiate labour and subsequently to effect therapeutic abortion. Subsequent to this, they were used to induce menstruation. Prostaglandins $F_2\alpha$ and E_2 are two of the naturally occurring prostaglandins which have been widely used clinically. More

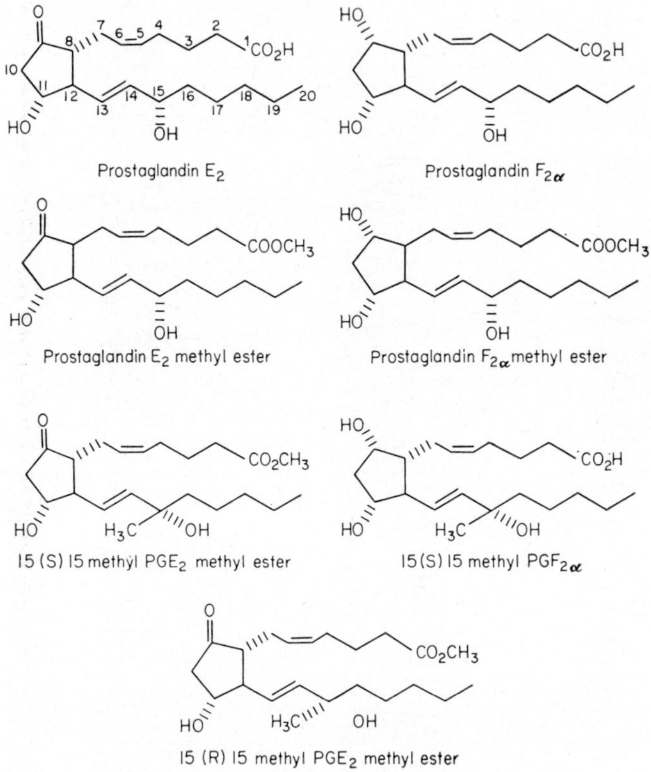

Fig. 2. Formulae of prostaglandin analogues.

recently, analogues have been used, namely the 15-methyl analogues. The formulae of these analogues are shown in Fig. 2.

Prostaglandins have been administered by several routes for inducing menstruation, namely intravenously, intramuscularly, subcutaneously, intravaginally and extraovularly. Prostaglandins produce a marked stimulating effect on the uterus (Fig. 3). Unfortunately they also cause a number of side effects, such as nausea, vomiting and diarrhoea, and less commonly headaches, blurring of vision and tachycardia. The analogues have an additional side effect of shivering and feeling cold. Side effects are dose-related, but some patients appear more susceptible than others.

The first report of menstrual induction was from Karim (1971). He reported the results of 12 patients, who were between 2 and 7 days late with their periods. Six patients had PG $F_2\alpha$ administered as a vaginal tablet at a dose of 50 mg on two or three occasions. A further

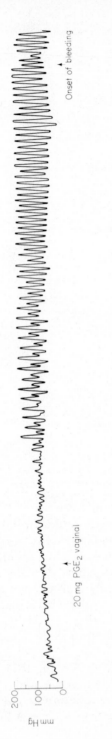

Fig. 3. Uterine activity following prostaglandin administration (5 weeks amenorrhoea).

6 patients had PG E_2 as a vaginal tablet at a dose range of 20 mg on two or three occasions. Vaginal bleeding occurred between 1 and 24 hours following the first dose. Eight patients had a positive pregnancy test before treatment and 11 patients had a negative pregnancy test after treatment. One patient failed to abort and required subsequent termination. Side effects were 4 cases of nausea and vomiting, 3 cases of lower abdominal cramps and 2 cases of heavy flow. These results were encouraging.

Sato and colleagues (1973) from Japan reported their use of PG $F_2\alpha$ vaginal tablets for incuding menstruation in 10 patients who were premenstrual between 2 and 14 days. The dose range was 25–50 mg. Menstruation was induced in 6 out of 10 patients. All patients had side effects.

Csapo and colleagues (1973) investigated the effect of intrauterine administration of PG $F_2\alpha$ in 22 patients. A single impact dose of 5 mg of PG $F_2\alpha$ was instilled into the uterus 12 days $\pm$ one after the missed menstrual period. Twelve patients were sedated and had uterine activity monitored. Ten patients were neither sedated nor monitored. Of the sedated group, 10 patients were aborted successfully. Three patients had nausea, or vomiting. All 10 cases who were not sedated aborted. One patient was reported to have had peripheral vascular collapse. This method appeared to be effective with minimal side effects. However, they recommended that all patients be sedated prior to administration as stomach cramps were often severe for the first hour following administration.

More recently Karim and colleagues evaluated the effect of the 15 (s) 15-methyl E_2 methyl ester for menstrual induction at a dose of 25–40 μg. Administration was 1 to 3 times daily. The results were an improvement over the naturally occurring compounds, in as much as the failure rate was less and the side effects were less. However, the presence of failures, which were of the order of 15 per cent, and the combined presence of side effects made the method far from acceptable as a method of contraception, although it could be an alternative to abortion.

Wentz and Jones (1973a) reported a transient luteolytic effect of PG F_2 when infused over an 8-hour period at a dose of 50 μg per minute, in the luteal phase of the menstrual cycle. Further to this study, they induced menstruation in 12 out of 13 patients who had missed their period by up to 14 days. (Wentz and Jones, 1973b) Four patients were not pregnant and 9 were pregnant. Four patients continued with their pregnancy but were curetted subsequently. Histological examination demonstrated damage to the gestation in each case.

In this study the plasma progesterones fell during PG administration whereas the plasma oestrogen levels were maintained, suggesting a transient luteolytic effect with a selective action on the luteal cells.

Whereas a post-conceptional drug for inducing menstruation appears to be a theoretical, acceptable method of population control, all reports have demonstrated some drawbacks and limitations of the method as a whole. These can be summarized as follows.

1. There is difficulty in establishing an accurate date of the last menstrual period. Up to 20 per cent of women either are not sure of their last menstrual period, or give dates which do not correlate with the size of gestation.
2. There is a technical problem of clinically establishing the size of an early pregnant uterus. This is especially difficult in obese patients.
3. The diagnosis of pregnancy is unreliable during the first 14 days of a missed period. A simple and more sensitive method of detecting pregnancy within a day or so of a missed period would be most welcome.
4. It is often difficult to get patients to a doctor at such an early stage. This is a matter of mass education and propaganda.
5. Because of the critical time of drug administration, a 7-days service should be employed. A person 10 days late with a period cannot be told "come back next week".
6. Side effects reported are often severe and are not conducive to repeat applications.
7. Subsequent bleeding is often erratic and the next period is not always predictable. This would make it difficult as a monthly method of birth control.
8. The failures present a problem. These would ultimately have to be terminated conventionally.
9. Follow-up is often difficult and patients—including failures—may not turn up.

In conclusion, prostaglandin administration as a method of fertility control, as it has been studied to date, is very appealing, but as yet has not proved itself as a simple and effective method for terminating early pregnancies. However, with improved technology, newer analogues may be more selective in action to cause termination of early pregnancy without side effects.

Menstrual Extractions

This is basically suction termination of pregnancy. In the first 2–3 weeks after a missed period, the gestation is small and may be sucked through a small-calibre cannula without prior dilation to the cervix. This method was popularized by Harvey Karman, an American psychologist. He devised a modification to a cannula known as the Karman curette or cannula. The 4 mm curette can pass through the cervix and into the uterus easily without dilatation. Suction can be applied by fitting a syringe on the cannula and pulling the plunger out, thus creating a vacuum inside the syringe. The plunger is kept out by a simple locking device. Movement of the curette up and down and rotating it through 360 degrees evacuates the uterus simply and speedily. The products are sucked into a syringe and can be seen and easily sent for histological investigation. No premedication or local analgesia is necessary (Karman and Potts, 1972). Marjolis and Goldsmith (1972) reported the average time taken to do this procedure to be 1 minute 55 seconds up to 6 weeks amenorrhoea, and 2 minutes up to 7 weeks amenorrhoea, with a range of 40 seconds to 4 minutes. Blood loss was on the average 14 ml up to 6 weeks, and 23 ml up to 7 weeks, with an overall range of 5 ml to 117 ml. Some patients experienced pain during the procedure and likened it to a severe period pain. Others found it painless. In 186 patients, failure to aspirate occurred in one patient who had fibroids. Two patients were non-pregnant and 3 patients had a pyrexia. In over 98 per cent no complications were observed. This method has now been successfully employed in more than 15,000 cases and is very simple, cheap and effective; it is associated with very few complications and causes minimal psychological trauma to the patient. It is an out-patient procedure and patients may go home within half an hour of the procedure. Problems associated with the method are minimal and include the usual difficulty in establishing the last menstrual period,

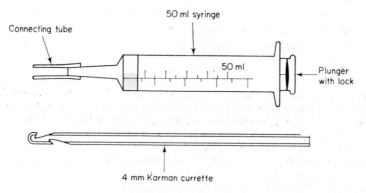

FIG. 4. Menstrual extraction.

obesity, a retroverted uterus and the stomach cramps experienced at the time of the procedure.

The 4 mm Karman curette is satisfactory up to 6–7 weeks of pregnancy. The 6 mm and 8 mm and more recently the 10 mm curette have now made it possible to perform suction curettage on patients up to 12 weeks gestation. The technique is basically the same, only an electric pump or a hand pump supplies the vacuum. Anaesthesia is with local anaesthetic. No dilation is usually necessary. If it is necessary, it is commonly performed under local anaesthetic. Lewis *et al.*, (1971) reported a series with very promising results. Because of the simplicity of the method, lack of necessity for general anaesthesia, and dramatic reduction in complications, it can safely be used as an out-patient procedure.

Abortion is at present the most widely used method of birth control throughout the world and it is now widely employed in this country. The numbers of patients being treated under the National Health Service are still rising. Fortunately the technological advances which have brought forward the Karman curette as a method of early termination of pregnancy may not only dramatically bring down the cost of abortion, but also dramatically reduce the complications and late sequelae of abortion. However for this to happen, the following recommendations are suggested, namely that:

1. more doctors should be trained to use these methods of early termination pregnancy as an out-patient procedure;
2. the general public should be made aware that this type of technology is available;
3. doctors' receptionists should also be aware of the advantages of referral early on; patients should not be told "bring a sample of your urine next week and we will get a pregnancy test done";
4. finally, General Practitioners should also be informed of the urgent need to refer patients early; this can be effective only if recommendation 1. is fulfilled!

References

Csapo, A., Mocsary, P., Nagy, T. and Kaihola, H. L. (1973). The efficacy and acceptability of the "prostaglandin impact" in inducing complete abortion during the 2nd week after the missed menstrual period. *Contraception*, **3**, 2, 125.

Karim, S. M. M. (1971). Once-a-month vaginal administration of prostaglandin E_2 and $F_2\alpha$ for fertility control. *Contraception*, **3**, 3, 173.

Karman, H. and Potts, D. M. (1972). Very early abortion using syringe as vacuum source. *Lancet*, **i**, 1051.

Lewis, S., Lal, S., Branch, B. and Beard, R. W. (1971). Out-patient termination of pregnancy. *Br. med. J.*, **4**, 606.

Marjolis, A. J. and Goldsmith, S. (1972). Early abortion without cervical dilation pump or syringe aspiration. *J. Reprod. Med.*, **9,** 5, 237.

Sato, T., Ami, K. and Matsumoto, S. (1973). Induction of abortion and menstruation by intravaginal administration of prostaglandin $F_2\alpha$. *Am. J. Obstet. Gynec.*, **116,** 2, 287.

Wentz, A. C. and Jones, S. J. (1973a). Transient luteolytic effect of prostaglandin $F_2\alpha$ in the human. *Obstet. Gynec. N. Y.*, **42,** 2, 172.

Wentz, A. C. and Jones, S. J. (1973b). Intravenous prostaglandin $F_2\alpha$ for induction of menses. *Fert. Steril.*, **24,** 8, 569.

Population Policies in the Developing Countries

C. M. STEWART

Government Actuary's Department, London, England

The serious situation which provides the background to the subject matter of this paper is too well known to require more than a brief mention. More than two-thirds of the world's population live in countries in which the level of economic development is a very long way behind that in the rest of the world. They are sometimes referred to as the less developed countries, but more usually as the developing countries, no doubt as an expression of optimism that the gap will be narrowed in future. However, it is not only the low level of development which distinguishes them from the more advanced countries. They are also characterized by a much higher rate of population increase—about $2\frac{1}{2}$ or 3 per cent a year, compared with about 1 per cent a year in the more advanced countries. It will be appreciated that a rate of increase of $2\frac{1}{2}$ or 3 per cent a year will double the population within a generation. The limited capacity of developing countries to absorb such rapidly growing numbers puts a great strain on them and impedes their economic advancement. My aim is to describe the extent to which governments in the developing countries, in recognition of this problem, have adopted policies directed towards reducing the rate of population growth.

The last time I studied this subject was in 1966 and it has been very interesting to see the change which has taken place in the past seven years. At that time I was able to discover only five developing countries which had unequivocally declared themselves in favour of a policy of family limitation and had introduced measures in their development plans to achieve this end. Those countries were India, Pakistan, South Korea, Tunisia and Turkey. Information on mainland China was hard to obtain, but the indications were that that country too should be included, making a total of six—which, with the separation of Bangladesh and Pakistan, has now become seven. However, in a number of other countries the government was actively supporting independent family planning associations so the spread of measures aimed at family limitation was wider than might have been supposed. According to the latest information currently available, by 1971 there were twenty-eight developing countries with an official policy to reduce the rate of population growth and, in a further twenty-six, family-planning activities were supported for other reasons. This is rather less than half the total number of developing countries but it includes most of the large ones so that it covers about five-sixths of the total population of these countries.

In 1966 it was not easy to collect up-to-date information on activities in all countries. The best source was the family-planning studies published from time to time by the Population Council in New York. However, the Population Council now publishes annually a Factbook presenting current information on national population policies and family-planning programmes throughout the world, so the problem is no longer one of searching for information but of selecting what is important from the fairly comprehensive summary tables now produced. These summaries show selected demographic, social and economic characteristics for individual countries, they describe each government's position on population growth and family planning activities and they also give detailed information on the operation of the family planning programmes. Although I have drawn on other sources for my purpose here it is fair to say that much of what was required was available in the Factbook.

The total world population in 1971 is estimated to have been about 3,700 million. Of this figure 1,100 million was in the more advanced countries and 2,600 million in the developing countries, comprising the whole of Africa, Asia and Latin America, with the exception of Japan, Argentina and Uruguay. The meaning of these large figures is difficult to grasp. It is therefore necessary to break them down and relate them to some figure which we do understand. For example, we know that the total population of the United Kingdom is between 50 and 60 million, much the same as France, Italy and West Germany. In the developing world, Nigeria, Mexico and what is left of Pakistan are about the same size. Bangladesh is rather larger, at about 75 million. Brazil is larger again with 100 million, the same as Japan, and Indonesia has about 125 million. Still larger we have USA with about 200 million and the Soviet Union with 250 million. Only two countries have larger populations than this; India with about 550 million, ten times the population of the United Kingdom, and China with 800 million. These last two taken together contain more than half of the total population of the developing countries.

Smaller than the United Kingdom, about two-thirds the size, with between 30 and 40 million, we find six countries in the developing world: Egypt, Turkey and Iran in the Middle East, and South Korea, Thailand and the Philippines in the Far East. These six countries, together with the eight larger ones mentioned above, contain nearly four-fifths of the total population of the developing world, so that consideration of population trends in those countries alone will give a good indication of the prospects for the developing world as a whole.

China

It has never been easy to obtain hard facts on the situation in China. However, it is now considered that, since 1962, China—this largest of all countries with a population generally agreed to number about 800 million—has qualified as one of the countries with an active policy aimed at family limitation. Premier Chou En-lai is reported to have said in 1964:

> We do believe in planned parenthood, but it is not easy to introduce all at once in China and it is more difficult to achieve in rural areas, where most of our people live, than in the cities. The first thing is to encourage late marriages . . .

Although the degree of official interest in family planning has varied from time to time the government continues to advocate late marriage and small families of two or at most three children, and to provide an active programme of contraceptive services, abortion and sterilization. The minimum legal age for marriage is 20 for men and 18 for women but marriage earlier than age 28 for men and 25 for women is discouraged. In view of the effectiveness of the propaganda media in China, who can doubt that what is advocated by the government will be generally accepted by the people?

To the sources of information on China we must now add *The Times*, following an interesting brief article from Peking which appeared only recently. It reiterated that the reasons for China's adoption of a family planning policy was not because of food shortages but in order to protect the health of the mothers and to ensure planned economic growth. It stated that birth control pills had been available since 1965. They were distributed free and had become widely available and very popular during the past four years. It listed other factors controlling population growth, mentioning male contraceptives, sterilization, abortion, prudery, lack of privacy, late marriage and separation of couples. The most interesting of these, to my mind, is prudery. It is reported that premarital intercourse and illegitimate births are considered to be so shocking that officials in China can barely be brought to discuss their existence, and an interpreter (to quote the article verbatim) "may go into paroxysms of embarrassment if asked to interrogate teenage girls on their marriage plans".

Birth and death rates for China were given in the 1970 Factbook but not repeated in 1971. Whether or not there is any significance in the omission, is not stated, for example a doubt as to their accuracy. However, for what they are worth they showed a birth rate in recent years of under 4 per cent a year and a death rate under 2 per cent, resulting in a population increase of about 2 per cent a year. These figures do not look unreasonable but, given the dynamic nature of populations, even if fertility could be substantially reduced, population growth in China would continue for many years to come.

One can illustrate this by reference to the situation in Hong Kong and Singapore, two very small territories with a combined population of only 6 million or so, a mere "drop in the bucket" so far as world population is concerned But both territories have for some time had strongly-supported family-planning programmes and did not, because of their small size, have a problem of reaching remote rural areas. As a result, their programmes have shown significant results more quickly than is likely to be achieved in larger areas. In the past ten years, the birth rate has fallen from nearly 4 per cent a year to about 2 per cent a year, which is quite dramatic. However, the death rate has also fallen and currently stands at only $\frac{1}{2}$ per cent a year, so that the total population is still increasing at about $1\frac{1}{2}$ per cent a year, in spite of the dramatic fall in fertility.

Crude rates of birth, death and natural increase require very careful interpretation if they are not to mislead. In a stationary population where the expectation of life at birth is 70 years, the crude death rate would be the reciprocal of 70, i.e. 1·4 per cent, and the crude birth rate would be the same. This is a simple arithmetical relationship which I find it very useful to remember. But no modern country is in this position because none has yet brought fertility down to replacement level. In the United Kingdom, fertility has in the past been only a little above replacement level, so the proportion of young healthy individuals in the population is only moderately in excess of what it would be in a stationary situation and the death rate is therefore only a little lower than 1·4 per cent—in fact, it is about 1·2 per cent. In Hong Kong and Singapore, however, because of very high fertility in the past, the age distribution of the population is very much younger than it would be in a stationary condition, thus producing a death rate at present of only $\frac{1}{2}$ per cent a year, or about one-third of what it would be in our hypothetical stationary condition. It will take many years of low fertility before the death rate will increase to anything like the size of the birth rate even at replacement level.

If one were to attempt a description of this situation in general rather than statistical terms, one could say that, because of high fertility in the past, the next generation of adults at the reproductive ages will inevitably be much larger than the present one, so that even if fertility were to be held at replacement level the size of the population would go on increasing for many years to come. It seems appropriate to interpolate these remarks at this point so as to put in perspective what a successful population policy for family limitation might achieve. An immediate reduction in fertility to replacement level might nevertheless mean that population increase would come to an end only a generation or two hence.

India

After China, the country with the next largest population is India, now with a population of 550 million. India was in fact the first country in the world to declare a policy for controlling population growth—as long ago as 1952—and successive economic plans have made increasing provision for implementation of the programmes. To begin with only experimental projects were established, based on the rhythm method of avoiding conception, followed by the creation of a family planning organization and a few training centres. Interest in the subject was promoted through mass education media and services were provided through clinics and hospitals. However, progress was very slow and it was only through sterilization, which received government approval in 1958, that much progress was made at all.

But by the end of the second five-year plan in 1961 it was realized that the programme had done little more than scratch the surface of the problem. In the third five-year plan the programme was therefore stepped up. The budget allocated more than ten times as much money as in the previous five-year plan. Apart from sterilization, the main plank of the programme was the use of condoms but this was expensive for such a vast population and required an enormous network of distribution centres to produce any real impact.

The arrival of intrauterine devices on the scene in 1965 changed matters considerably. Because of the clinical and administrative advantages of this method over sterilization an effective mass programme now seemed feasible. A special Committee was formed "to review what additions and changes were necessary as a result of the greatly altered situation . . ." A Family Planning Committee was set up at Cabinet level and the Ministry of Health was renamed the Ministry of Health and Family Planning. The programme was reorganized with the District as the pivotal point and the whole operation made more purposeful and effective than hitherto.

In the fourth five-year plan (1966–71) the budget allocation was again increased—to about 200 million US dollars, which sounds a lot of money but it worked out at only 8 cents per head a year for a population then approaching 500 million. It was planned, over the five years, to complete 20 million IUD insertions, 5 million male steriliz-ations and to have 10 million effective users of traditional contracep-tives. By a continuation of these methods it was hoped to reduce the birth rate from about 4 per cent to $2\frac{1}{2}$ per cent a year by 1975. At last it seemed that the Indian Family Planning programme had gained some of the momentum necessary if it was to have the required impact in a fairly desperate situation.

The planned reduction of the birth rate to $2\frac{1}{2}$ per cent a year by 1975 proved to be too optimistic and the target was subsequently changed. The birth rate in 1969 was still more than 4 per cent a year and the new aim was to bring the rate down to $2\frac{1}{2}$ per cent by 1980 or 1982 with an intermediate milestone of 3·2 per cent by 1974. But once again it is *The Times* newspaper which has the last word. Recently it reported from Delhi that, as part of a plan to curb inflation, the budget allocation for the family planning programme in 1973–74 was to be cut by two-thirds. This announcement brought a statement from senior officials at the Ministry of Health and Family Planning that the reduction would make it impossible to achieve the planned reduction in the birth rate to $2\frac{1}{2}$ per cent a year by the end of the decade. This is clearly a major setback.

Indonesia

Indonesia has only recently established a national policy with the aims of informing the people about family planning, providing services and reducing the birth rate. Although announced in 1968 it has not yet made much inroad in this very large country, with a population already 125 million and increasing at something between 2 and $2\frac{1}{2}$ per cent a year. However, in 1970 a government Board was established to coordinate the work of the several ministries and private organizations concerned in the family planning programme, and fees are no longer charged to persons accepting services. These and other measures have been adopted to help expedite the programme. Oral contraceptives and IUDs are being provided in roughly equal numbers and it is hoped to achieve a target of 6 million acceptors during the 1971–75 five-year plan.

Brazil and Latin America

Brazil has the next largest population in descending order of size with 100 million, but we can conveniently consider Mexico, with about 50 million, at the same time. These countries have the two largest populations in Latin America and, like a number of smaller countries in that region, their populations are increasing at more than 3 per cent a year, about the highest rate found anywhere in the world. Neither country has, however, adopted a national policy of family limitation. Strong religious and cultural attitudes have generally inhibited Latin American governments from adopting such programmes. Because of low population density, official and public opinion has focussed more on the manpower needs to achieve national development and the colonization of empty areas and there has therefore been hesitation towards adopting policies of family limitation. However, the very rapid rate of population increase appears now to be influencing opinion in favour of family planning and another factor has been the very large number of illegal abortions in the area. Statistics of the numbers of abortions are, for obvious reasons, lacking or at best unreliable, but the incidence is considered to be very high and to be resulting in widespread maternal deaths and ill-health. Humanitarian reaction to the misery this causes is providing an important stimulus to the liberalization of attitudes towards contraception in the whole area.

The United Nations Fund for Population Activities reports that it is now—with government approval—supporting family planning projects in twenty-two countries in the region including the launching of a large-scale programme in Mexico in 1972. The groundwork is therefore being laid which might later facilitate the adoption of national policies by those countries if they should so decide. Should this happen, it will follow a pattern set in many other countries where the initial impetus to organized family planning was provided by private organizations or groups. Among these, family planning associations, women's associations, the medical profession, universities and foundations have had a marked impact on population policy developments and on organized governmental activities. In some countries the private arrangements became so large and well organized that they formed the nucleus of the national government programmes which were established. This is one form of nationalization that we are unlikely to see opposed by anyone and if the various ventures now being pursued in Latin America should in time pave the way for the adoption of nationwide government programmes this would be a very desirable outcome.

Pakistan and Bangladesh

In 1960, when these two countries formed a single nation, a family planning programme was drawn up and arrangements were made for its implementation as part of the 1965–70 five-year plan. The target was to make services available to all fertile couples (estimated to number about 20 million) and to reduce the birth rate from 5 per cent to $4\frac{1}{2}$ per cent by 1970, with further reductions in later years. Implementation of the plan was concentrated on IUDs and on conventional contraceptives, principally condoms and foam tablets. Studies of acceptability were made concerning the possibility also of using oral contraceptives.

Bangladesh is now a separate country with a population in the region of 75 million. The government has confirmed its interest in reducing the rate of population growth and in supporting a national family planning programme, although such activities are not expected to receive important attention until recovery from the war of secession is complete. The main noticeable difference from the family planning programme in Pakistan is that well over 1 million sterilizations have been carried out in the region which is now Bangladesh but relatively few in what is now Pakistan.

The population of Pakistan is now a little over 60 million. The birth rate appears already to have fallen to below $4\frac{1}{2}$ per cent a year by 1970 and it is hoped to bring this down further to $3\frac{1}{3}$ per cent by 1975, with 31 per cent of fertile couples using contraceptives by then. During the period 1970–75 oral contraceptives are to be introduced to the programme and a new team of specially trained literate men and women brought in as full time operators to replace the village midwives who have hitherto played a major role in carrying the programme to every part of the country. If the planned reduction can be attained, this will be a major achievement in a relatively large country in the developing world.

Nigeria

So far I have mentioned seven out of the eight developing countries which have populations as large as or greater than the United Kingdom. Five in Asia have firm government policies aimed at controlling population growth; the other two, in Latin America, have not. The eighth country is Nigeria with a population of about 56 million, the largest in Africa. Nigeria has a national population policy, dating from only last year, to implement a family planning programme, but not with the aim of reducing the rate of population growth—although that would be a very valuable by-product in a country whose population is increasing by about $2\frac{3}{4}$ per cent a year at present, and it would be even more rapid but for the very high death rate.

At present it is the private Family Planning Council of Nigeria which predominates in the field of family planning but the government intends to implement its own population policy and programme and to coordinate all external aid for family planning activities. The Second National Development Plan (1970–74) concludes that the population problem in Nigeria is not so serious as to call for panic action, because the economic prospects for the country are so promising. To quote the plan verbatim:

> What seems appropriate in the present circumstances of Nigeria is for Government to encourage the citizens to develop a balanced view of the opportunities for individual family planning on a voluntary basis, with a view to raising the quality of life of their offspring. Facilities are to be designed to protect mothers, on a long range basis, from repeated and unwanted pregnancies, as well as to enable parents to space their children for better feeding, clothing and education. . . . During the Plan period, the Government will pursue a qualitative population policy by integrating the various voluntary family planning schemes into the overall health and social welfare program of the country. Families will have access to information, facilities and services that will allow them freedom to choose the number and spacing of their children.

The emphasis is thus, literally, on family planning rather than on control of population growth, so that Nigeria is not one of the twenty-eight officially antinatalist countries to which I referred earlier, but one of the twenty-six which support planning activities for other reasons.

The actual programme, which is still very new, is based mainly on IUD insertions and on oral contraceptives, with rather more people favouring the former than the latter. No targets have been set for achieving any specific decrease in the birth rate, presumably because that is not the purpose of the programme. But there can be little criticism of a programme aimed at the building of happy healthy families and reducing maternal and infant mortality.

Egypt, Iran and Turkey

Next in descending order of size are the six countries mentioned as having populations of between 30 and 40 million, about two-thirds the size of the population of the United Kingdom. All six have one thing in common, a declared population policy for controlling population growth.

First, the three Middle East countries.

In Egypt the policy to reduce the rate of population growth was established in 1965 by a presidential decree. The target was to reduce the birth rate by one point a year for the next ten years, i.e. from about 4 per cent to 3 per cent. The annual rate of population increase is already under $2\frac{1}{2}$ per cent a year which is not so desperately large as in many other developing countries. In the period up to 1971 there were over 1 million acceptors of family planning services, roughly two-thirds favouring oral contraceptives and one-third IUDs.

In Iran, the official policy dates from 1967 and is aimed at reducing the rate of population growth from 3·2 per cent to 1 per cent a year over the next twenty years which is a very ambitious plan. The oral contraceptive is by far the most important method used at present.

In Turkey there had for many years been an anti-contraceptive law, but in spite of this the Economic Planning Board began working in the early 1960s towards legislative changes and programme planning. This far-sightedness saved valuable time when government policy changed. In early 1965 Turkey repealed the old laws forbidding abortion, sterilization and the importation and sale of contraceptives or the dissemination of information about them; a family planning law was passed to implement a national programme through the Ministry of Health and Social Assistance, with cooperation from the Army and other government agencies.

Popular approval of contraception and of government involvement in a national programme had been clearly established beforehand by a sample survey covering more than 5,000 married persons in 240 villages and 70 large centres of population. The wishes of the Turkish people were thus made clear and in 1965 the government responded by becoming one of the earliest to embark on a national programme of family planning, but it is still too early to look for evidence of progress in terms of a reduction in births. The IUD is the main method used in the programme, but oral contraceptives are obtained through the private sector and account for much current practice. The rate of population growth is currently about $2\frac{1}{2}$ per cent a year.

Of particular interest in the Turkish situation was the survey carried out beforehand in order to assess the wishes of the Turkish people. Such surveys are very important if a programme is to be implemented with the maximum success and there is a special table in the

Population Council Factbook listing those countries which have conducted KAP surveys and quoting some of the results. The derivation of the name KAP is not difficult to discover: K is for Knowledge of contraception, A is for Attitude to contraception, and P is for Practice of contraception, the things that those planning a programme most need to know concerning the persons at whom the programme is to be directed. You might say that K, A and P are the three Rs of planning a programme.

South Korea, Thailand and the Philippines

The other three countries in this group are all in the Far East.

South Korea was the third Asian country, after India and Pakistan, to organize a national family-planning programme. Since it was introduced in 1961 the progress has been rapid and tangible results can be observed. Things really got moving in 1963 when there was an energetic "mass enlightenment" campaign which resulted in more than one million couples registering their interest in family planning and accepting a trial supply of condoms or foam tablets. Tests were also started on IUDs. It was reported that Korea was manufacturing all its own supplies of contraceptives, sufficient to keep pace with its expanding programme and even for exports to other countries. Targets were set, and achieved, for IUD insertions, male sterilizations and users of condoms, etc., and the programme now also supplies oral contraceptives.

The overall target was to reduce the birth rate from 4 per cent to 3 per cent a year in the space of ten years and the latest statistics indicate that this has pretty well been achieved. The rate of population growth has fallen to about 2 per cent a year.

In 1970 Thailand approved a family planning programme with the objective of reducing the annual rate of population growth from 3 per cent to $2\frac{1}{2}$ per cent over a period of five years. IUDs and oral contraceptives are available in government hospitals and health centres. In the same year, 1970, the Philippines also introduced legislation providing for a national programme of family planning which would respect religious beliefs, with the purpose of meeting the grave social and economic challenge of a high rate of population growth. In this case the target is set not by reference to birth rate or the rate of population increase, but with the intention of enrolling half of the eligible couples in the country as acceptors of IUDs or oral contraceptives by the year 1976. In both countries, it may be noted, KAP surveys had been conducted in order to pave the way. It may also be noted that, at 3·4 per cent a year, the Philippines have currently just about the highest rate of population growth recorded anywhere in the world.

General Situation

I have now described, fairly briefly, the situation in the fourteen largest developing countries which nevertheless together contain nearly four-fifths of the total population of the developing world. To attempt similar descriptions for all the other smaller countries would result in meaningless repetition. However, for the developing world as a whole the picture is fairly clear. The past seven years have seen an expansion and strengthening of the family planning movement, with more and more governments adopting and running national programmes, and tangible results are now being seen in reductions in the birth rate in many countries, particularly in the Far East.

Some Genetic Consequences and Problems of the New Biology

J. A. BEARDMORE

Department of Genetics, University College of Swansea, University of Wales

Introduction

What is the new biology? As I started to write this paper I asked a number of colleagues from various biological disciplines how they would define the "new biology". It rather surprised me to receive a variety of answers which had only one common attribute—they were all evasive!

Luria (1965) portrays the new biology as depending largely upon "molecular genetics—a key to biological progress". The achievements of molecular genetics are described as the establishment of the following:

the genes as discrete durable units of heredity;
the genes as located in linear assemblages in chromosomes;
the relationship between genes and characters and the nature of pleiotropy;
the chemical nature of genes;
the chemical nature of replication;
the chemical nature of the message the genes despatch.

Macfarlane Burnet (1971) implies that the "new biology" is synonymous with molecular biology, but that is a very ill-defined term and its existence as a discrete discipline is doubted by many biologists.

My own view is that the term should certainly include the elements of Luria's list but also other notable advances in e.g. ecology, ethology, immunology and endocrinology and the advances in knowledge following the development of techniques for resolving the fine structure of cells and molecules such as electron-microscopy, chromatography and electrophoresis. Although there are very important roots

from earlier years the majority of these advances have materialized in
the last two decades.

I intend to discuss genetic implications of the new biology under the
following heads:

Genetic change and genetic damage—the input of new genetic variation
from mutation and mutation-like processes.

Genetic disease—its recognition, treatment and consequences of successful treatment.

Genetic influences on life span and consequences of increasing the mean
age of death.

Population New Biology—considerations of the nature of human gene
pools and considerations relevant to a population policy.

Mutation

As a result of new (and not so new) biology, the permanent heritable
changes in genetic material known as mutations are now fairly well
understood although estimates of the frequency of spontaneous
mutation in man are still far from perfect. Mutations arise as a result of
stochastic errors in the replication of the genetic material or are
induced by mutagenic agents of which the first to be discovered was
ionizing radiation. The risks arising from increases in mutation rate
due to exposure to ionizing radiation have been repeatedly pointed
out particularly since the advent of the Atomic Age. Fortunately in the
present climate of test ban treaties the genetic risks from fall-out are
very small although the population exposure to ionizing radiation in
industry and in diagnostic medicine is increasing.

It may be inferred that the level of the mutational load carried by
man is increasing from radiation causes though we do not know by
how much.

Recent decades have seen an increasing usage of many varieties of
synthetic and novel molecules for the flavouring, colouring and stabil-
ization of food, in domestic, industrial and pharmaceutical preparations for the control of disease in man and other organisms, for
growth control in economically significant plants and animals and for
other purposes. Recent advances in biological knowledge have shown
that some of these molecules have potent effects upon the genetic
material. For some and perhaps many of these, hindsight shows that this
could have been expected for they were selected for use in the first
place because of the profound and fundamental effects they have upon
living systems. The fact that many have been put into use before the
mechanism of their action is fully understood means that we are right

to adopt conservative attitudes towards the widespread use of new chemicals. In this context, it is, of course, not unimportant that for most of these agents man has had no evolutionary history of exposure in which to evolve cellular systems giving some protection against such alien molecules. It is, at present, impossible to estimate the extent of genetic damage arising from this source although it may be significant. The two most obvious problems in this connection are lack of information as to the level of doses administered and the lack of knowledge of the metabolic transformations which may be undergone by such molecules before they have a chance to reach the gonads. (This of course leaves aside the question of resultant somatic mutations, neoplastic occurrences and generalized physiological derangements which may take place after ingestion.) Some substances, not in themselves mutagens, may give rise to mutagenic substances in appropriate conditions. Nitrite, widely used as a food preservative, is worthy of note in this connection and cyclophosphamide is another substance in this category.

Whatever benefits the population derives from using the vast range of molecules of which Table I lists only a small sample, we must be aware that there is a risk of adding to our load of mutations from direct chemical mutagenesis and perhaps also from synergistic effects such as might take place between certain molecules and ionizing radiation. Experiments of the type discussed by Neel (1972), in which populations are screened for protein variants at many loci, are needed to indicate the magnitude of these additional mutations.

This addition to the mutational load is expected to result in an increase in genetic disease both genic and chromosomal and some phenotypic change in quantitative characters. It is also worth noting that there may also be similar genetic hazards caused by living organisms themselves, notably some viruses. Chromosome breaks have been reported in patients following infection by hepatitis virus, and following use of vaccines containing live virus for measles, rubella and mumps. Mycoplasma also produce chromosome breaks in tissue culture (Nichols, 1972). As viruses are used in some countries for insecticidal purposes there is clearly a potential risk that they could act as environmental mutagens.

Genetic Disease

It is now widely recognized that a considerable fraction of the burden of disease suffered by a Western urbanized society is influenced by genetic factors in one way or another. This fraction may represent possibly some 40 per cent (Childs et al., 1972) or so of paediatric cases

TABLE I

Examples of molecules producing genetic hazards

Substance and Reference	Use	Mutagenic when tested on
DDT[a]	Insecticide	Rat, human tissue culture
Vapona[a]	Insecticide	Onion and bean root tips, *E. coli*
Tepa[a]	Water-repellent, adhesives, crease-resistance	Mouse, *Neurospora*, *E. coli*, T_4
Organomercurials[a]	Fungicides	*Drosophila*, Man
Ethylene oxide[a]	Fumigation	*Drosophila*, *Neurospora*, Maize
Mecoprop[b]	Herbicide	Yeast
Mitomycin C[a]	Anti-neoplastic	*Drosophila*, *Vicia*, human leuko-cytes
Chlorpromazine[a]	Tranquillizer	*Mouse*
Nitrite →HNO_2[a] + nitrosamines[c]	Food preservative	HNO_2—*E. coli*, Yeast, T_4, Neurospora Nitrosamines—*Arabidopsis*
Cyclophosphamide[d] →unknown derivatives in blood and urine	Anti-leukemia drug	Mouse, yeast

(a) Fishbein (1972); (b) Parry (1973); (c) Veleminsky and Gihner, (1968); (d) Siebert (1973).

(or 25 per cent of hospital beds, Thompson and Thompson, 1966). The most striking and genetically simple are the inborn errors of metabolism such as phenylketonuria (PKV), cystic fibrosis of the pancreas, Huntington's chorea and haemophilia. As the great majority are recessive, the incidence of most genetic diseases is much higher in marriages of relatives than in marriages of unrelated individuals. More complex inborn errors are those due to the interaction of two or more loci and those caused by irregularities in the normally very high fidelity of chromosome replication and segregation as, for example, in non-disjunction of chromosome pair No. 21, the cause of most cases of Down's syndrome.

Genic Disease

The demonstration that proteins are coded for by genes showed that most simple inborn errors are due to defective enzymes, and this has stimulated efforts to identify the specific components of the metabolic pathways involved. Alleviation of the condition might then follow as has happened in the case of phenylketonuria by a dietary restriction, by transplantation of tissue of an appropriate genotype (Mukherjee and Krasner, 1973) or by a supply of the relevant enyzme. However, in the latter case ensuring that the preparation is stable and can reach the right tissues may present problems (O'Brien *et al.*, 1973). However, where the genetic block is of a regulatory kind rather than at a structural locus there may well be possibilities for the relief of genetic disease by the supply of the controlling protein. In some growth anomalies, for example, it would seem that the identification and timely supply of an appropriate hormone could provide more or less complete repair. The relief of genetic disease presents many difficult problems; undoubtedly one of the widely held hopes for the future is that genetic addition to, or substitution in, the affected individual's genome in at least some of his tissues can take place. The knowledge gained from transduction experiments with bacteriophages by which portion of bacterial chromosomes can be moved from one strain to another is relevant here. Equally the recent success in nuclear trans-plantation and in fusing genomes of different species and hence producing new genomes might indicate pathways which could turn out to be fruitful in the long run. These and other techniques for genetic improvement are considered later.

Let us now ask: what are the populational consequences of applying knowledge, in whatever form, to the alleviation of genetic disease? Relief of individual distress is important but other consequences may follow. Under stable conditions the frequency in the population as a whole of a deleterious recessive gene is at an equilibrium governed by a balance between mutation giving rise to the recessive gene and selec-tion removing such genes from the population.

Now if the selective disadvantage is reduced to a small value, as will happen in cases of genetic disease to which an effective remedy has been applied, the equilibrium value will increase. The incidence of phenylketonuria in the UK is estimated to be about 4×10^{-5} (Munro, 1947). Such individuals are homozygous for a recessive gene pk and the frequency of this gene is then 0·0063 (i.e. 0·6 percent). Before successful treatment, the selective disadvantage attached to PKU may be assumed to be 100 per cent. If the selective disadvantage is reduced to, say, 20 per cent and no artificial restriction on the repro-duction of affected individuals is assumed the frequency of pk rises ultimately to 0·014. That is, it is more than doubled with a consequent five-fold rise in the frequency of affected homozygotes. However, the progress towards the new equilibrium is extremely slow, so much so that twelve centuries would be required even to double the incidence of PKU (Crow, 1967). That this change is so slow depends very largely upon the fact that the mutant gene is very rare. For other genetic diseases the outlook may be less favourable. Cystic fibrosis of the pancreas occurs in 1 in 2,000 births (Carter, 1972), with a gene frequency of 0·022. The disease, until recently, led to death in early life. If the reproductive fitness of homozygotes approaches that of unaffected individuals there will be a more rapid increase in cases than with PKU This amounts to something over 25 per cent increase in five generations and a doubling within fifteen generations. Cystic fibrosis is not a typical example because it is the commonest recessive disease but it is clear that the alleviation of genetic disease as a result of progress in the new biology may result in genetic consequences with appreciable social and economic costs attached to them.

The problem with dominant genetic disease is at once simpler, because all genes are revealed (except where there is incomplete penetrance), and more difficult because, following repair or alleviation, the increase towards the new equilibrium point is much more rapid. The rate of increase is proportional to the amount of selective disadvantage attached to affected individuals.

Let us assume in the case of the effectively lethal condition, achondroplasia, that the disease could be 90 per cent repaired by intervention. The frequency of affected individuals (1/10,000) would then rise within a few generations to a new equilibrium with about ten times as many affected individuals as before (Crow, 1967). For sex-linked recessives the situation is intermediate between that for autosomal recessives and dominants as the frequency of the mutant allele is directly reflected in the frequency of affected males.

We may therefore conclude that the application of new biological and medical knowledge to the alleviation of genetic disease will, in the absence of any constraints on reproduction, produce a significant increase in the incidence of genetic disease over the next few generations although for the majority of conditions this will be extremely small.

Chromosomal Disease

By this we understand those conditions brought about by losses, re-arrangements or addition of chromosomal material, usually brought about by breaks or by non-disjunction. Most chromosomally unbalanced zygotes are lethal at very early stages of development and so pose no long term major problems. Some however survive as, for example, in individuals with Down's syndrome and those with the syndromes associated with non-disjunction of the sex chromosomes. A number of ways of reducing the incidence of such chromosomal disease are available following partly from greater understanding of the causes of non-disjunction, partly from recent technical developments such as fluorescent banding techniques, and partly from the availability of methods such as amniocentesis by which the chromosomes (and, some few of the genes) of foetuses may be assayed well before term. It seems unlikely, as others (Thoday 1972) have pointed out that remedies for the exceedingly complex disturbance of normal function occasioned by chromosomal imbalance will be forthcoming and as these individuals are effectively sterile no increase in frequency resulting from improved survival is expected.

Genetic Influences on Life Span

It is convenient to separate discrete genetic disease from more subtle genetic influences on life span and reproductive success. The new biology of gerontology lies largely in the future as the molecular mechanisms responsible for ageing are still largely unknown. However, various lines of evidence including radiation experiments, chromosome analysis and analysis of protein sequences suggest that some, and possibly much, of the ageing process is due to mutational events of some kind (Medvedev, 1967).

The new biology of the last few decades has been partly responsible for the greater average life expectancy now enjoyed in Britain and similar countries. This has occurred, of course, partly as a result of the development of antibiotics whereby infectious diseases, instead of being responsible for a substantial fraction of deaths, have disappeared from the list of the top ten killers in 1970.

As Meade indicates earlier in this volume, the age structure of the population has been considerably changed so that those who are sixty-five or older are now some four times as many as in 1900. This in itself has no necessary genetic consequences although it might conceivably be instrumental in delaying the age at marriage in the case of some individuals. However, it seems very probable that the increased survival of individuals who in other times and places would have died at younger ages, though for non-specific reasons, may well have genetic consequences. This follows from the fact that the reproductive success of some of these individuals is higher in the contemporary environment and from the argument that susceptibility to almost any disease is likely to be distributed normally in the population with part of the variation under genetic control, as is established for diseases like duodenal ulcer or essential hypertension (Clarke, 1970). The genetic consequences of such interference with what would happen under a "more Natural Selection" cannot be predicted with any confidence although they might be quite significant. This is because we have no idea at present whether such selection, when it acts on a quantitative character, is instrumental in changing the frequencies of multiple heterozygotes relative to homozygotes or whether simpler effects of a directional kind operate as in the case of phenylketonuria discussed above.

Population New Biology

One of the most striking advances of the new biology has been in establishing the immense range of genetic variability found within populations of a wide range of species. This work using immunological, electrophoretic and other molecular techniques has established that human populations characteristically have at least one third, and probably more, of their structural loci polymorphic (Harris, 1970); that is there are at least two alleles normally present in the population at appreciable frequencies. The consequences of this knowledge are manifold:

the idea that the average genotype is almost completely homozygous is demonstrably false;
there are clearly no identical genotypes except in the case of members of an identical twin pair;
there is no such thing as the normal genotype—only a large range of normal genotypes;
the notion of pure races cannot reasonably be accepted any longer.

In the average individual at least 7 per cent of the loci in his genome and probably 20 per cent or more (Harris and Hopkinson, 1972) are heterozygous. The number of different combinations of genes possible, if man is assumed to be polymorphic at 4,000 loci with only two alleles at each locus, is 3^{4000}. This is an immense number, far exceeding the number of people who have ever lived. Thus the range of genotypes now living represents only a limited sample of all possible genotypes but at the same time this range is composed of individuals who are all genetically different from each other.

The extent to which races differ genetically is a matter of some controversy but thanks to the development of serological and electrophoretic studies firmer foundations are now being given to the debate. Recent work shows clearly that there is a very considerable overlap in genetic constitution between the races of man. Using a crude measure based on data for twenty-six loci (Cavalli-Sforza and Bodmer, 1971) I have calculated that the average difference for polymorphic loci in one or both races would seem to be about 18 per cent between caucasoid and negroid races. As not all loci are polymorphic this estimate of the difference may be biased, most probably by being too high and perhaps 6–12 per cent could, very tentatively, be considered nearer reality.

The evidence briefly summarized above is an important part of a greater body of fact which has been responsible for a considerable shift in the philosophical approach to biological phenomena. This change is from typological thinking to populational thinking which, although not yet complete, has had profound effects in many disciplines and not least in human biology (Dobzhansky, 1968). Mayr indeed says "the replacement of typological thinking is perhaps the greatest conceptual revolution that has taken place in biology".

The reasons why such a vast quantity of genetic variability for proteins, blood groups and similar characters is maintained in populations are, for the most part, still unknown. For a few of these polymorphisms it is clear that they are adaptive, for example in that the population acquires a partial genetic resistance to a disease such as malaria (Allison, 1964). Experiments with other species tend to suggest that some polymorphisms have adaptive significance in relation to environmental variables like temperature, density and enzyme substrates (Beardmore, 1970). However, based largely upon theoretical considerations some workers consider that some, possibly much, of the polymorphic variation in proteins is non-adaptive (King and Jukes, 1969). These polymorphic loci are interesting in another connection— that of quantitative inheritance. There is a growing body of opinion which considers it likely that most of the genes of quantitative inheritance are genes at polymorphic loci detected by, or expressing, pleiotropic effects upon the character in question (Birley and Beardmore, 1972). Taking this view, when other, more primary effects of these genes are examined they will be seen to be genes with orthodox, Mendelian properties. It must be said however that this is an area in which the new biology has not yet advanced as far as many of us would like to see.

Whatever the nature of the genes influencing quantitative characters may be, the significance of these genetic factors for the present discussion is that many important aspects of physical and mental constitution are normally distributed in the population and of particular concern to us are attributes like intelligence and those behavioural traits associated with the social relations of man. Evidence is accumulating that the extent of genetic control of important personality-influencing organs like the pituitary and the adrenals (Shire, 1968) is considerable but the characterization of the genes involved is slow. Work of this kind, of course, could be of considerable significance for the resolution of the arguments in areas where biology and sociology overlap such as those of the pro-and anti-Jensenites (Jensen, 1973).

A Population Policy

It now appears that countries such as the UK are rapidly approaching a state in which the means for effective control of population size are freely available, due to the development of biological devices on the one hand and social attitudes on the other. In developing countries the population problems are of a different order as several contributors to this symposium have pointed out. Even though goals and policies for population quantity can be explicitly stated the matter of population quality is considerably more problematical. This is not a new problem and almost forty years ago H. J. Muller, pioneer of mutation studies, in a prescient little book called *Out of the Night* (Muller, 1935) argued that there are good reasons for man purposefully to control the composition of his own gene-pool.

This question has been extensively debated over the years, particularly in terms of the relationship between fertility and IQ and both Thoday and Carter have discussed it recently from somewhat different standpoints. I do not want to go over the ground again but I believe we should accept that Muller's essential thesis was right. We are on the way to producing a population policy but almost all of the discussion centres solely upon the question of total numbers. As I see it there is a logical paradox in insisting that population size must be controlled but that there need be no control of the rates of reproduction of individuals. Indeed, one could develop an argument which predicts that a population policy founded upon this basis could result in an increased frequency of genes influencing anti-social behaviour. The preceding sentences should not be taken to mean that I know exactly what should be done but I am sure that within the next generation some formal consideration of population quality, as well as of quantity, will need to form part of any governmental policy on population.

Such a policy is obviously likely to involve a stepped-up programme of research into cheap, efficient genetic screening for chromosomal aberrations and for heterozygotes for deleterious recessive genes (Carter, 1972), measures to discourage inbreeding and measures to discourage the reproduction of at least some of the patently genetically handicapped.

Euphenic measures must presumably continue to be used but if these represent a significant and increasing share of the demand on available resources considerable ethical problems, of the type discussed later in this volume by Pole, may arise.

What positive eugenic measures should be worked for? This question cannot be answered on a scientific basis at present. However, it seems reasonable to suppose that important qualities such as satisfaction, physical and mental well-being, creative initiative and national wealth would be significantly different in populations with different gene-pool compositions.

With the increasing complexity of life in technological, social and other aspects, I think it reasonable to argue that more consideration should be given to such matters than has been the case in the past.

Possible approaches towards genetic improvement are outlined in Table II. Many of these are still only remotely probable and the prospects of useful genetic engineering seem, on various grounds, to be over-rated. Objections to cloning have been recently summarized (Carter, 1972) and my own view is that the most generally used techniques are likely to be those named in Sections 3 and 4. As the right hand side of the table indicates there are many unknown factors and I do not pretend that in trying to set out positive and negative features I have done more than make a few fairly obvious points.

So much for methods; in order to make *decisions* we need much more relevant information. Unfortunately we are still far too ignorant of the extent and nature of the genetic factors influencing behavioural attributes and I trust that I may be forgiven for remarking that I have the impression that many of those working in the behavioural sciences are reluctant to see that union between their own and the biological sciences which must ultimately come about if we are to arrive at a full understanding of the nature of man in all its aspects. I do not know why this reluctance exists, but the dogmatic pronouncements about "what makes man what he is" made, on occasion, by influential people in relation to such important matters as educational theory and practice serve only to underline heavily the need for full and objective experimentation and collection of relevant data.

Much more extensive, and intensive, systematic study of human populations, utilizing the techniques both of biology and the social sciences, should be undertaken. I am thinking here of the kind of work being carried out by Gibson and his collaborators in which they have succeeded in identifying at least one polymorphic blood group locus as being associated with the normal variation in IQ (and hence with social mobility) in a sample from a rural population (Gibson *et al.* 1973).

The association, real or imagined, with various political movements

TABLE II

Possible pathways towards genetic improvement

Method	Application (potential or actual)	Positive features	Negative features
GENETICAL ENGINEERING			
a. Transformation type	Gametes, zygotes	?	Non-specific; low efficiency
b. Transduction type	Gametes, zygotes	?	Control of virus difficult
c. Nuclear transplantation	Zygotes	?	Cellular damage problems
d. Nuclear hybridization	Zygotes	?	Difficult; unbalance of genome
e. Mosaic individual (two different nuclei)	Zygotes, organs*	Probably simpler than a–d	?
CLONING	Adult tissues Twin zygotes	Rapid production of "good" types	Social and ethical
GENETIC SCREENING			
a. Heterozygotes for recessives	All newborn	Population record	Cost
b. Zygotes *in utero*	Suspect zygotes	Abortion potential, early treatment	Medical risk
ARTIFICAL SELECTION			
a. Differential fertility	Adult population	Phenotypic consequences more predictable	Social and ethical
b. Sperm from selected donors	As (a) plus sperm bank	Phenotypic consequences more predictable	Social and ethical
c. Implantation of selected zygotes in "foster" mothers	Zygotes from suitable matings	?	Social and ethical

* Unless the gonads were affected, this unlike all other methods of genetical engineering would not influence what genes were passed on to the next generation.

has significantly handicapped the sensible discussion of eugenic policies up to now whilst euphenic progress tends to be taken for granted. I hope that we can begin to break away from this inhibiting influence so that rational and humane consideration of the scientific, social and other implications of expanding biological knowledge in all its aspects can take place.

References

Allison, A. C. (1964). Polymorphism and natural selection in human populations. *Symposia on Quantitative Biology*, **29,** 137–149. New York: Cold Spring Harbor Laboratory of Quantitative Biology.

Beardmore, J. A. (1970). Ecological factors and the variability of gene pools in *Drosophila. Evol. Biol.* Supp. 299–313.

Birley, A. J. and Beardmore, J. A. (1972). Manifold large selective effects in an enzyme polymorphism. *Fifth European Marine Biology Symposium*, 81–100. Padua: Piccin.

Burnet, F. M. (1971). *Genes, Dreams and Realities*. Aylesbury, England: Medical and Technical Publishing Co.

Carter, C. O. (1972). The new eugenics? In *Population and Pollution*. Edited by P. R. Cox and J. Peel. London: Academic Press.

Cavalli-Sforza, L. L. and Bodmer, W. F. (1971). *The Genetics of Human Populations*. San Francisco: Freeman.

Childs, B., Miller, S. M. and Bearn, A. G. (1972). Gene mutation as a cause of human disease. In *Mutagenic Effects of Environmental Contaminants*. Edited by H. E. Sutton and M. I. Harris. New York and London: Academic Press.

Clarke, C. A. (1970). *Human Genetics and Medicine*. London: Edward Arnold.

Crow, J. F. (1967). Genetics and medicine. In *Heritage from Mendel*. Edited by R. A. Brink. University of Wisconsin Press.

Dobzansky, T. (1968). On genetics and politics. *Social Education*, **32,** 142–146.

Fishbein, L. (1972). Pesticidal, industrial, food additive and drug mutagens. In *Mutagenic Effects of Environmental Contaminants*. Edited by H. E. Sutton and M. I. Harris. New York and London: Academic Press.

Gibson, J. B., Harrison, G. A., Clarke, C. A. and Hiorns, R. W. (1973). Existence of relationsip between I. Q. and ABO blood groups. *Nature*, **246,** 498-499.

Harris, H. 1970. *The Principles of Human Biochemical Genetics*. Amsterdam, London: North Holland.

Harris, H. and Hopkinson, D. A. (1972). Average heterozygosity per locus in man. An estimate based on the incidence of enzyme polymorphisms. *Ann. Hum. Gen.*, **36,** 9–20.

Jensen, A. R. (1973). *Educability and Group Differences*. London: Methuen.

King, J. L. and Jukes, T. H. (1969). Non-Darwinian evolution. *Science*, **164,** 788–798.

Luria, S. E. (1965). Directed genetic change: Perspectives from molecular genetics. In *The Control of Human Heredity and Evolution*. Edited by T. M. Sonneborn. London: Collier-Macmillan.

Medvedev, Z. A. (1967). Molecular aspects of ageing. In *Aspects of the Biology of Ageing*. Edited by H. W. Woolhouse. London: Cambridge University Press.

Mukherjee, A. and Krasner, J. (1973). Induction of an enzyme in genetically deficient rats after grafting of normal liver. *Science*, **182,** 68-69.

Muller, H. J. (1935). *Out of the Night*. New York: Vanguard Press.

Munro, T. A. (1947). Phenylketonuria: Data of 47 British families. *Ann. Eugen.*, **14,** 60–88.

Neel, J. V. (1972). The detection of increased mutation rates in human populations. In *Mutagenic Effects of Environmental Contaminants*. Edited by H. E. Sutton and M. I. Harris. New York and London: Academic Press.

Nichols, W. W. (1972). Mutagenicity of biologicals. In *Mutagenic Effects of Environmental Contaminants*. Edited by H. E. Sutton and M. I. Harris. New York and London: Academic Press.

O'Brien, J. S., Miller, A. L., Loverde, A. W. and Veach, M. L. (1973). Sanfilippo disease type B: Enzyme replacement and metabolic correlation in cultured fibroblasts. *Science*, **181,** 753–755.

Parry, J. M. (1973). The induction of gene conversions in yeast by herbicide preparations. *Mutation Res.*, **21,** 83–91.

Shire, J. G. M. (1968). Genes, hormones and behavioural variation. In *Genetic and Environmental Influences on Behaviour*. Edited by J. M. Thoday and A. S. Parkes. Edinburgh: Oliver and Boyd.

Siebert, D. (1973). A new method for testing genetically active metabolites: Urinary assay with cyclophosphamide (Endoxan, Cytoxan) and *S. cerevisiae*. *Mutation Res.*, **17,** 307–314.

Thoday, J. E. (1972). The right to reproduce. In *The Future of Man*. Edited by F. J. Ebling and G W. Heath. London: Academic Press.

Thompson, J. S. and Thompson, M. W. (1966). *Genetics in Medicine*. London: W. B. Saunders.

Veleminsky, J. and Gihner, T. (1968). The mutagenic activity of nitrosamines in *Arabidopsis thaliana*. *Mutation Res.*, **5,** 529–531.

The Galton Lecture 1973:

Population Prospects and The New Biology

PETER R. COX

Government Actuary's Department, London, England

Demographic topics figure so prominently in the calendar of the Eugenics Society nowadays that it is easy to forget that they were not always such a major preoccupation. In nearly sixty Galton Lectures thus far they have received first priority of attention only twice: in 1935, Carr-Saunders took for his title "Eugenics in the Light of Population Trends", and in 1950 Parkes spoke on "Some Aspects of the Population Problem". On each of these occasions there was a strong current of topicality beneath the choice of subject—first in the concern over the new-found prospect of a declining population, and secondly in the quieting of that concern following the publication in 1949 of the Report of the Royal Commission.

Some Galton Lecturers have included more limited reference to population developments in association with other matters of interest, such as human biology, and in recent years there has been an increasing tendency to deal with more than one theme at once: a tendency which properly reflects the multi-disciplinary nature of bio-social science. Indeed, when biology and one of the social sciences overlap, their common ground normally includes some reference to the numbers, growth, distribution or analysis of the population. While therefore the proximate cause of my choice of title is the need to ventilate a subject which will fit in well with the Symposium programme, there is perhaps also a more general reason for considering the demographic implications of certain of the scientific developments that are taking place today.

Moreover, public interest in population matters is probably more intense now than it has been at any time since 1950. The scene has changed in the past twenty years. The moment seems to have arrived for the third of the Galton Lectures to give its attention primarily to demographic questions. Only in such circumstances would I feel justified in opening my thoughts to public scrutiny in this way. In so far as it may be necessary for me to touch on biological or medical matters it is on the understanding that I have no right to claim any professional expertise on those matters. It gives one confidence, however, to remember that not only does the new biology affect population but also population through its sociology can now react to some extent on the course of biology, for instance by exerting an influence on the way in which money is spent on research; moreover, both reactions take place with the aid of an important catalyst—human behaviour, a subject on which no one seems to be inhibited from making his feelings generally known.

Before I start to make any sort of detailed comment upon relationships of this kind it is clearly incumbent on me to explain what I understand "the new biology" to mean. It is not long, historically, since the very word "biology" itself was coined, at the beginning of the nineteenth century, to mark a stage in an extended process of discovery and development which has already had some profound effects on population. In the light of the many changes this process has wrought, can it be plausibly argued that recent innovations are so exceptional as to stand out prominently from the scientific trend line? Some writers argue that we are about to experience a real break-away, so much so that research needs to be carefully controlled. But do they underestimate the length of time required for real success in most new discoveries, for testing and validation, for bringing to manufacture on a large scale, and for widespread adoption by the public? Perhaps the only thing which is developing in an unprecedented manner at the present time is our awareness of the potential long-term social effects of science?

The new biology thus represents, maybe, nothing more than the current segment of a steadily upward trend line in scientific advance. To say this is not to give a specific definition, and it might be more helpful to point to particular developments—say those listed in the programme of the current Symposium—and to state that it is the sum of these which constitutes our required definition. But for practical reasons this list is necessarily incomplete. Perhaps I should therefore enlarge on it by saying that, in recent years, a lot has been heard of devices for prolonging life, for instance, transplants when a vital organ is worn out; of drug-induced mood-control for the alleviation of mental suffering; of researches into the process of ageing and into the inheritance of longevity; even of methods for preservation of a corpse against decay in the hope that someone will some day find a means of restoring life to it. Much has been said about the means for greater control over unwanted births—contraceptive pills, improved techniques of abortion, prostaglandins and the like. Still more novel are studies connected with the elimination of sterility, and with forecasting or controlling how a foetus will develop. Then there is the work designed to make it possible for a foetus to grow outside the womb. Finally there is genetic engineering—the manipulation in the laboratory of the basic elements of heredity, obviously of exceptional interest for our Society, but at the moment little more than a concept which could be put into practice only in the more distant future.

This is a motley mixture of developments, some already with us, not very effectively, today and some no more than an idea for the twenty-first century, though Rattray Taylor (1968) has given hostages to fortune on a big scale by predicting just when each one of them will begin to affect all our lives. But without doubt they add up to something important. Their impact on population is not always evident at a first glance, and different biological novelties will undoubtedly have very different effects, so much so that each one will need to be considered separately.

It is, however, relevant to ask whether the interactions between the new biology and the population constitute a matter of sufficient importance for such a lecture as this. Is not all the laboratory activity likely to have a much more immediate and interesting impact on our habits, our society, our law, our comfort and our politics? AID may influence the birth rate much less forcibly than the way in which it impinges upon the rules of inheritance. Transplants and mood control may not increase longevity greatly but they may in the end create doubts as to just what sort of an individual the patient is after the treatment. Apparatus which is available only for a few raises ethical questions in the selection of who shall benefit and who not. It is problems such as these which lead to pleas for a check to "progress" in the laboratory. Nevertheless, some of the items on our list can affect population directly and significantly; and the words of Walter Bagehot in 1876 are still worth quoting: "The causes which regulate the increase of mankind are little less than all the causes, outward and inward, which determine human action."

I feel, therefore, that there is justification for my title, even though the subject is unprecedented. I believe that one can usefully discuss the "new biology" of the past as a guide; contemplate its probable effects; show what the population situation is today as a consequence of this and other factors; indicate what are the demographic prospects for the next thirty years; and, finally, speculate how the future might be altered as a result of the discoveries which, so far as we can see today, may be expected to be made or developed during or after that period.

I feel that there is no compulsion upon me to look further ahead than this; but it would not be new for a demographer to do so. Addressing the Population Association of America at its Dinner Meeting, Bourgeois-Pichat (1972) said that "in 200 years so many things can happen". He drew attention to an article entitled "Transplanted Nuclei and Cell Differentiation", in which the author (Gurdon, 1968) explained that, after fertilization, the egg can be removed and replaced by an ordinary cell taken from any individual of the same species: the process of gestation then continues with the ordinary cell and when it reaches its term the child born is the twin of the donor of the ordinary cell. Gurdon had caused this to occur in frogs. Bourgeois-Pichat explored some of the possible consequences if it was found, in due course, that the process could be applied to human beings.

In a not too serious exposition he envisaged such outcomes as (i) a gross imbalance of the sexes of the new-born in some years, influenced by astrological predictions; (ii) the extension of the cult of personality so far as to produce millions of twins of the current political leader; and (iii) such problems as those of naming twins of the new type and indeed of deciding what their age was. Curiously enough, this speaker did not enlarge on what the size of the population would be. Almost any answer could have followed, and this explains why his exposition had to be couched in flippant terms.

The biological studies I listed earlier can be divided, so far as their reaction on population changes are concerned, into two classes: on the one hand, those related to births, and what precedes or prevents them; on the other hand those connected with survival or death after birth. Thus some advances primarily affect fertility and some primarily affect mortality. It could hardly be otherwise, for these are the essential elements in demography. The only further basic factor, migration, is determined mainly by forces not of a biological character. In a parallel manner, two influences play an important part in what is discovered by means of research, or more meaningfully what emerges in a form suitable for practical use: the desire of all people for better health and longevity; and the wish of many to be able to control the number of their offspring. Inasmuch as the aim of a small family arises from a consciousness of the disadvantages of population pressure, it may be said that the demographic situation feeds back upon the development of biology. In a more direct and important sense, the principal ingredients of population change can exert some effect on the way in which science moves ahead, through the medium of public demand.

These statements are self-evident, yet some part of their whole truth is often omitted by those who wish to startle us with visions of the future. Usually the feedback effects are neglected: some new finding is to alter all our lives, and we are to submit to it without any reservation at all—that is the dramatic presentation. Yet there could, in theory, be a reaction sufficient to nullify completely any deleterious consequences. In the days of horse-drawn transport, deaths resulting from road accidents occurred at a frequency which seems surprisingly high to us now. If, in the age of the motor car, we were as careless as people then seem to have been there would be good deal more carnage than there actually is today. The death rate from accidents involving vehicles has increased by less than 100 per cent in the last fifty years while the density of traffic must have grown tenfold. People, and their institutions and laws, have to a large extent adjusted themselves to the new situation.

We are now near enough to 1984 to be confident that the world will not be anything like that predicted by Orwell in the 1940s, Brech in the 1960s, or any other utopists (whether eutopists or kakotopists). What normally happens in practice is that the outcome is neither so bad as was feared nor as good as one might have hoped. Often the change is much slower than would have been thought possible. A number of examples can be cited in which the progress of medicine has been retarded, for various reasons, although it is everyone's desire that a cure should be effected wherever possible. Where people's aims are more diverse and complex, as in the control of fertility and family size, even slower change, moreover with fluctuations, can be expected.

Writers of science fiction either disregard such a lag or avoid it by choosing a setting which is far ahead in time. We cannot usefully discuss population prospects in these ways; such value as projections have applies only to the next fifty years at most, and their relevance today diminishes from everything to nothing as the year to which they refer advances from 1975 to 2025. During this period, any influences exerted by recent biological discoveries will work only in a gradual way, speculation about the course of which will call *inter alia* for the expertise of a sociologist, for the attitude of the public will be very important.

Sir John Charles (1964) asked the question "Who in 1900 would have imagined that the death-rate from typhoid fever in England and Wales which was then 216 per million population would be 16 in 1920 and 4 in 1940?" There is, however, another kind of question that can equally well be put and is perhaps more relevant to my theme: "Who in the year 1910, when salvarsan had just been discovered by Ehrlich, would have expected that deaths from syphilis, then running at around 2,000 a year in this country, would still be as numerous as 500 a year 40 years later?" Even in 1970 some 200 deaths were recorded in England and Wales. (see Fig. 1.) True, some delay in the eradication

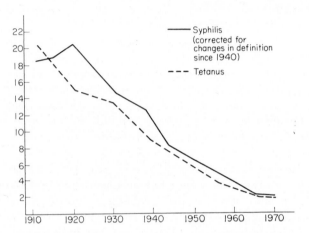

Fig. 1. Numbers of deaths per annum from syphilis (in hundreds) and from tetanus (in tens) England and Wales

of the disease should have been thought likely in respect of the time required:

  (i) for the drug salvarsan to be manufactured in sufficient quantity;

 (ii) for knowledge of its value to spread to all doctors; and

(iii) for cases of consequent circulatory and other impairments to clear themselves by death;

but these could hardly require all of sixty years to take total effect.

It does not appear that analytical studies of the history of the decline in mortality from specific causes such as this are capable of tracing all the reasons for the course of the figures but, in general terms, the literature indicates that salvarsan is not, in fact, always curative (though it prevents the spread of infection); it is indeed now replaced by other chemotherapeutic agents as the treatment of choice. Just as important, many affected persons do not consult their doctors soon enough to obtain the full benefit of the discovery.

Similarly, tetanus mortality is still with us although it is over fifty years since effective anti-toxin became generally available. The number of deaths, 200 in 1910, was still 100 in 1940 but is now reduced to the region of ten a year. With this disease, the process of scientific discovery has been gradual, from recognition of its infectious nature in the 1880s to the use of induced paralysis, in recent years, to ease the severe muscular tension which can cause death. These two examples show how a new biological discovery, which it is to everyone's advantage without reservation to use as quickly and fully as possible, can be very slow in having its full effect, because of the need for supplementary discoveries, because of ineffectiveness not originally suspected, or because of persisting public ignorance, carelessness or fear. Indeed, as Fig. 1 shows, the rate of progress is similar for both diseases.

Social inequalities can cause an appreciable wagging in the tail-end of a process of improvement in the death-rate from a disease. Thus Brewer (1971) listed a number of infectious diseases the incidence of which lingers on in the USA from causes which might be thought highly unlikely to operate in such a generally prosperous country: insufficient nutrition accounts for some tuberculosis; poor housing and overcrowding allow rheumatic fever to continue; racial discrimination in the health services is alleged to be responsible for the prevalence of trachoma in some areas. The elimination of these residual elements is much more a matter for economic and social justice than for the new biology, which can contribute little, except perhaps through the discovery of new remedies which are easier or cheaper to apply and so can penetrate more widely to all classes.

It would be absorbing indeed if I could show for each important disease what I have given for syphilis and tetanus, or if I could attach a similar series of figures to each major new discovery in biology and then add together all the results. This is not, however, generally possible. To quote McKeown (1965),

Biologists... have been interested particularly in the behaviour of individual infectious diseases and a considerable literature has been devoted to discussions of possible reasons for the decline of mortality from tuberculosis, smallpox ... and other infections. The biologist has not had the incentive of the economic historian to explain the behaviour of mortality as a whole. .... Medical achievement has not been a theme of medical history in the way that population growth has been a theme of economic history.

Even so, the two examples I have quoted encourage one in the belief that something of value can perhaps be extracted for my present purpose from the history of the last hundred years, even if it amounts to no more than a few quite general conclusions; these may help us to adopt a more reasonable attitude to the apparent problems and prospects for the near future. Let us look briefly, therefore, at certain points of time, starting with 1870, and assess, as far as possible, what the population situation then was, and what thinking people were saying about it, both considered in relation to what might be termed, if necessary with some stretch of the imagination, the "new biology" of the time. What actually happened subsequently can be compared with what seemed at the time to be likely.

The population of Britain in 1870 numbered 26 million. It was growing rapidly, and had increased from 18 million in 1840. The birth rate was thirty-five per thousand and had probably remained constant for a generation although the official statistics record a small rise. The death rate was about twenty-two per thousand, and this too had not varied much since 1840. Although one infant in three died before reaching reproductive age, there was a net reproduction rate of nearly 1½. (See Fig. 2.) So little did there appear a prospect of a change in the general trend that it seems to have occurred to hardly anyone to make a projection of the population. Clearly, Malthusian checks were not effectively in operation and growth would continue. Yet in the sphere of biology many highly significant developments had been

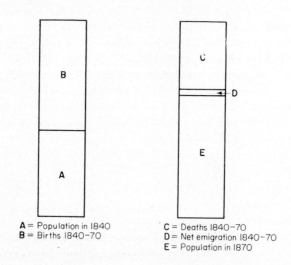

A = Population in 1840
B = Births 1840–70

C = Deaths 1840–70
D = Net emigration 1840–70
E = Population in 1870

Fig. 2. Population growth, 1840–70, Great Britain

taking place: the existence of cells had been discovered and a theory of germs had been formed; antisepsis had been advocated, and a clinical thermometer constructed. All these must surely be accepted as contributing a radical new biology in their day. Of more immediate impact, the need for sanitation had been established and much practical progress in this sphere was under way. Contraceptive devices had been developed and were about to be given a powerful advertisement by the Bradlaugh-Besant trial. These, to me, can also be included under the head of the new biology.

Judging by the literature of the times, which Banks (1954) has analysed so fruitfully for us, the aspects of population on which public attention was then focused were mainly economic ones. Poverty and its relation to large families assumed much importance—as a question for the individual more, perhaps, than for the nation. While, therefore, people were thinking and talking meaningfully about certain population questions, they apparently did not pay much heed to the potential influence of the new biology of the day, or foresee the effect it was to have. Even so, the general climate of opinion, in the middle classes, was becoming suitable for a big change.

If we now transfer our attention to the year 1900, we find that the British population total had reached about 37 million, and this is indeed what, in 1870, might have been assessed as being likely on the basis of growth in a geometrical progression from the 1870 numbers at the 1840–70 pace. The margin between the birth rate and the death rate had remained unchanged; yet both of these had in fact fallen substantially, by five per thousand (see Fig. 3). We are now at a point of time at which some of the oldest books now in the Eugenics Society's Library were published, and it is naturally of interest to see what can be deduced from these about the way in which thinking people were reacting to the changes. It does not seem as though the developments caused any special stir and indeed there is no real reason for expecting that they would have done so. Clearly, it was good that the death rate was falling; it showed the advance of civilization. The decline in the birth rate was regarded, no doubt, as a phenomenon reflecting the common sense of thinking people in managing their affairs in a society of increasing prosperity. In the heyday of British imperial power, the population was expanding in what must have appeared an entirely appropriate fashion.

Historically, this period is of special interest to members of the Society because Galton's eugenic theories were being developed, out of the new biology of such men as Huxley and Darwin. It seems very likely that the books our predecessors then purchased for the Library

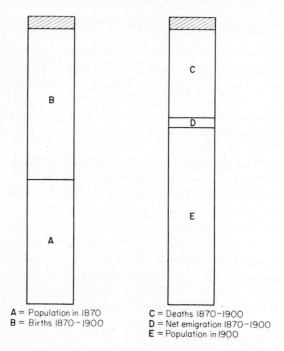

A = Population in 1870
B = Births 1870–1900

C = Deaths 1870–1900
D = Net emigration 1870–1900
E = Population in 1900

Fig. 3. Population growth 1870–1900, Great Britain. Shaded areas show excess of expected births and deaths 1870–1900 over actual, if expectation is calculated on basis of experience in 1840–70.

would have a bias towards the benefits of birth control; but it must be expected also that these books would argue in favour of the discussion of population problems and prospects in a scientific manner. If their content in this respect is thin, as it is indeed, then we can safely conclude that concern over population prospects was not at all prominent in public life generally. If a demographic prediction had been considered worth while, it must surely have disclosed an expectation that by 1930 Britain would have a total population of 54 million.

Meanwhile, biologists and medical men had been busy creating new things. During the last thirty years of the nineteenth century, the tubercle bacillus had been identified. The value of sanatoria had been revealed and many built, and it was recognized that good diet was important for a cure. X-ray diagnosis was just arriving. Progress had been made with smallpox vaccination, and in the study of other infectious diseases too. But there had been as yet little practical effect from these developments, as is evidenced by the infant mortality of the day—still 15 per cent in the first year of life. Advances had, however, been made in other directions, particularly in cardiology. Even so, it was a different age from the present. L. G. K. Starke (1952) said that

> he would like to meet one of the million people whose life history was recorded, say, in English Life Table No. 7 . . . such a person . . . still lived in a world of hansom cabs and horse buses; he had escaped both world wars . . . he had never heard . . . of wireless, the aeroplane, penicillin, the atom bomb, national insurance or anything else that had happened in the past 45 years.

According to McKeown (1965), therapy has been directly responsible for advances in the health of the nation only from the second quarter of the twentieth century onwards. Certainly, by 1935 the crude death rate had fallen to 12 per thousand—only one-half of its mid-nineteenth century level, and relatively lower still if allowance is made for the change in the age-distribution to an older population. Infant mortality, too had been halved. The new biology of the nineteenth century was now having its effect in full measure, but only after a lag of some fifty years.

If I may now turn to the period 1900–35: among the most famous life-preserving discoveries of this time were insulin, penicillin, a vaccine against yellow fever, and the treatments for syphilis and tetanus to which I have already alluded. Other notable advances were made in the fight against infectious disease. In 1935 it proved possible to isolate a virus for the first time. Important discoveries concerning human dietary needs were made, and the principal vitamins were identified. On other aspects of human biology, Asher and Zondek developed a method of testing for pregnancy, while oestrogen and progesterone were found. Developments in the theory of fundamental particles paved the way for the future science of molecular biology. Few of these new developments, however, had any significant effect on the current size, trend or quality of the population. For instance, the recorded death rate from diabetes actually rose, even after standardization for age, though better diagnosis no doubt contributed to this.

Nevertheless, the demographic situation was changing rapidly, with a decline in fertility which brought the British birth rate down from thirty per thousand in 1900 to only sixteen per thousand at the end of the period. The two-child family arrived, and growth of numbers slowed down. Instead of the 54 million that would have been forecast in the year 1900 there were only 46 million (see Fig. 4). To these dramatic changes the new biology contributed little directly, but perhaps much more indirectly. As our Galton Lecturer said last year (Meade, 1973):

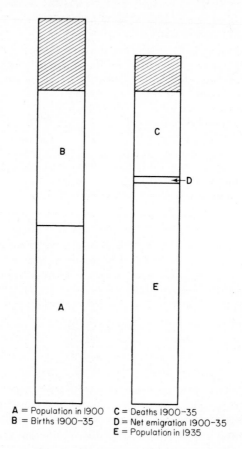

A = Population in 1900   C = Deaths 1900–35
B = Births 1900–35   D = Net emigration 1900–35
                         E = Population in 1935

Fig. 4. Population growth 1900–35, Great Britain. Shaded areas show excess of expected births and deaths 1900–35 over actual, if expectation is calculated on basis of experience in1870–1900.

What will happen to human society over the next half century depends upon a very complicated network of feedback relationships between demographic developments, industrial and economic developments, technological developments, biological and ecological developments, and psychological, political and sociological developments.

A network such as this cannot spring into being suddenly; it must have been already in existence—even if in a less complex form—for some while, certainly since the beginning of the present century; the contribution of one particular element to the general outcome cannot be precisely identified.

The impetus to population prediction which had hitherto been lacking was now provided, powerfully, by the developments illustrated in Fig. 4. Books and papers on the demographic problem appeared and they contained, indeed were based on, demographic forecasts. Some of them are in the Society's Library, but I need hardly consult it, because the spirit of the times is still fresh in my then impressionable mind. Remembering the War of 1914–18 and fearing a worse one to come, and disheartened by economic stagnation, people did not find it impossible to believe that the will to reproduce might indeed fade away almost completely. By 1971, the experts said, the total population of Britain might very well be smaller than in 1931, and falling steadily. (In the event, it rose by over 20 per cent and is now still rising.) In the light of this failure to predict, it is not surprising to find that the vein in which most of the authors wrote is now heavily varicosed, with its emphasis on such outmoded topics as lebensraum, qualitative decadence, and the national burden of dependency in old age. The remedies attempted by politicians of the day, such as race-hygiene, banning the production of birth-control materials, and so on, seem somewhat nauseating now. The demographer, with isolated exceptions, was the prisoner of his time, and unable to rise above it.

To conclude this brief historical survey I have to make some reference to the events of the period since 1935. But I need not say very much, because many of them are fresh in people's thoughts. Our newspapers and journals remind us frequently of the existence of combinations of antibiotics, of new vaccines, of transplants of organs and of groups of organs, of medically-induced multiple births, and other iatrogenic novelties. Pills, coils, abortion techniques, AID, and genetic counselling have materially enriched our capacity for controlling the quality and quantity of reproduction. The infant mortality rate is down to one-quarter of its value in 1935. Yet the crude general death rate, and the birth rate too, are only at about the same levels as they were 40 years ago. Some diseases are indeed on the increase. What, if anything, can we deduce about the inter-relationships between population trends and the new biology of this time? Here are a few pointers which I believe to have some significance now, and to derive from all the developments of the past hundred years.

First, while the new biological advances can have immediate and indeed striking effects upon particular individuals, or on special categories of people, their influence on current demographic trends is hardly perceptible. True, infant mortality has responded quickly but the effects of improved survivorship are submerged by the larger trends and fluctuations in birth rates. The pace of improvement in the death rates in childhood was quickened when chemotherapy and penicillin

arrived—as I found to my cost, having made some mortality projections just before this became apparent from the statistics (see Fig. 5).
But children's chances of survivorship were in any event very good
before this happened, and the effect on the future population size is
almost negligible. At adult ages, an increased incidence of some forms
of fatal disease has worked against therapeutic gains in other directions.

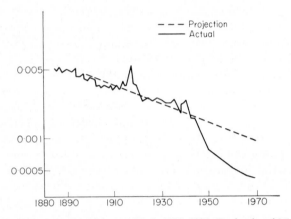

Fig. 5. Death rates for males aged 5–9, 1880–1970, England and Wales.

Secondly, biological and associated scientific discoveries, acting
alongside and through the medium of economic and social changes,
can influence population trends profoundly, after an appreciable time-
lag. I have already given some medical examples; but the existence of
a factor of delay, in varying degrees, can be seen in other aspects of the
subject. The way in which the contraceptive pill has been gradually
adopted in the USA (the proportion of married couples using it has
risen from zero ten years ago to one-third today) is an example;
another is seen in the degree of acceptance of the practice of contraception generally in the Far East (which is still slight in Indonesia but has
grown to nearly one-half in Taiwan in the past 20 years). Much that
has happened, however, is clearly an indirect result of the work of
Freud, more than half a century ago, and this is one reason why I have
included associated scientific discoveries under this head.

Thirdly, it is open to people to accept or reject the use of new
treatments and devices, and the altered way of life that they often
imply. Birth control, accepted in France in the eighteenth century and
in the USA in the early nineteenth, was, in the main, rejected by the
British until 1870. Here was a piece of new biology which conflicted

sharply with a value-system. In the end the value-system gave way, gradually, but only perhaps because people saw, in the social and economic circumstances, more utility in the new than in the old *modus vivendi*. Recently, there has again been much questioning of the notion that all scientific developments must be assumed to be beneficial, and an insistence on a more prolonged process of testing before new devices are put generally into use.

Fourthly, non-biological changes, such as those of a social or economic character, may exercise an influence on population which confounds the effect of biological developments. Increased consumption of alcohol, tobacco, sugar and fats, made possible by economic prosperity, has worked against the prolongation of life, and has partly succeeded in the process. It has now been argued that the elimination of fibrous residues from food has had a similarly baleful effect (Burkitt, 1973). Indeed, scientific advances may themselves act in a conflicting fashion: greater longevity may well have been a cause of the fall in the birth rate, through the medium of the economic cost of supporting non-working dependants, young or old.

Fifthly, non-biological influences can be much more striking and immediate in their impact on population than biological ones. The recent trend towards younger marriage and a quicker reproductive turnover is an example; though we cannot analyse the causes in detail, it cannot reasonably be supposed that better health in infancy and childhood is the major factor at work. The generally good physical quality of the population today owes much less to eugenic notions than to improved social measures—though in this respect it is not impossible that the relative importance of the two types of influence might be reversed in the future. One day, perhaps, society will call upon the biologist to achieve certain specific objectives, and to leave untouched those lines of inquiry which could lead in "undesirable" directions.

Sixthly, and finally in this analysis, it has not so far proved to be possible to forecast most demographic changes with any accuracy. This lack of success is surely the direct result of the confusion of influences to which I have drawn attention and of the unpredictability of delays and checks caused by people's reactions. Indeed, the very publication of population projections can itself be the cause of reactions which could remove some of the likelihood that the future will work out as expected. (The unfortunate outcome of this particular conclusion is that the lessons which can be drawn from this survey of the recent past are unlikely to be of great help in discussing the probable future of the population).

When population problems and policy were debated in the House of

Lords on 26 April 1972, Lord Zuckerman argued that the main requisite for a population policy is "information which would derive from a proper analysis of the changes in fertility rates". He continued: "We know what brings about falling mortality rates in different age groups, but we know all but nothing about the factors which, over the ages, have changed fertility rates in different societies and in different groups. We know about the correlation with economic status and with education; we know about female employment, about incentives and disincentives. What we do not know is how they work, if they work." In this, I think, he is broadly right; he made, indeed, about the most useful contribution to the whole Debate; but he has not given any real clue as to how his proper analysis can be achieved. The ideas which have been developed, over the past few decades, for effecting it are not bearing much fruit at the present time. Until the 1930s, in Britain, we had little to go on, in the way of comprehensive statistics, except the crude birth rate. The Population (Statistics) Act of 1938 gave us the means of studying in detail, by statistical means, the variations that occur in the birth rate between parents with different numbers of children, at different ages, and of different lengths of time married. What one tends to find, however, is that when a fluctuation in experience occurs it is of the same character in all these respects; the same thing happens for young and old, and for those with large and small families, and so the analysis is unspecific and tells us little of the true causes.

The next step adopted by the demographers, mainly in the USA, was to make local studies in which an increased array of correlates was incorporated. Fertility differences by religion, occupation and psychological and other characteristics were the object of attention. Here too, however, temporal changes seem to affect all groups in much the same way. Few important fertility differentials were isolated, and those of significance, e.g. religious disparities, are not of much help in predicting the future. After this came some more direct approaches to the problem: first, the survey of ideas and ideals on family size; but people do not, in general, carry out their ideas nor do they live up to their ideals. Later we have had the "family intentions survey", in which newly-married couples are asked to say how many children they expect to have. Tests show that, in the aggregate (though not in individual cases), the couples do accurately predict what they, in the event, will allow to happen. But the predictive quality of such studies is very limited in character; they give us little more than a glimpse for the next five years ahead. In five years' time most of the children of these couples will have been born and a new cohort of couples will be starting family life who, at the time of the survey, were too young to have formed any useful idea of their future intentions.

What comes next? I have not seen many new proposals. It occurs to me, however, that as we are still not finding out what it is that influences people to change the fertility rate so much in a short time we should now try to combine the merits of the analytical and the predictive study: to couple, in other words, the recording and testing of intentions with the recording and testing of influences. In this way we can perhaps find out also what it is that causes individual couples to vary their plans from the original intention; that should be useful, for while such limited predictive success as intentions surveys have rests on a balance of errors they can hardly be regarded as being based on a really firm foundation.

This will not be easy. It requires a longitudinal approach, spread over several years, in which each of the subject couples would need to keep a diary noting down their situation, thoughts and feelings at frequent intervals. In the first instance, clearly, a pilot survey is required, in which those studied would be specially chosen for their reliability as witnesses to themselves rather than for their general representativeness. Later, if apparent success was achieved in this way, the procedure could be extended over a wider range of couples. In some degree Peel (1970, 1972) has started along these lines: in his Hull marriage survey he showed that many young couples revised downwards their originally-intended number of children because they found in practice that the task of rearing children was more laborious, absorbing and costly than they had supposed it would be. More analysis along this direction seems practicable.

Prognostications of future population are not intellectually rewarding because of the imponderables. They do not offer any certain prospects of successful achievement. Nevertheless they are much in demand, and without doubt demography is a subject worthy of study. From this impasse there are two escape avenues:

(i) confine one's research strictly to the past and leave it to others to draw their own conclusions as to the changes to come;

(ii) discuss the future imaginatively, without any reference to past events, which are regarded as irrelevant.

Both of these avenues have their pitfalls. On the one hand, as Von Schlegel remarked, "A historian is a prophet in reverse"; even his findings can still be discredited by posterity. The doomster, on the other hand, will probably be forgotten long before posterity has had a chance to check his predictions; his work will be more quickly submerged by the clamour of the next round of scaremongers.

The main argument in favour of the medium-term demographic projection, based upon the latest available census data and the measured experience of the recent past, is that a population has a momentum of its own; because of its age-structure, in some degree it contains the blueprint for its own future. Moreover trends in mortality and fertility rates are not totally devoid of continuity in time. So long as one's horizon is strictly bounded, so long as every care is taken to stress the uncertainties, and so long as the work is continuously monitored and frequently revised, there is something of value in this type of activity to set against its evident defects.

This is the justification for the British official projections executed by the Government Actuary's Department and published annually. The methods used and the bases adopted are generally in accord with what is done in other countries. In the remainder of this Lecture I shall refer briefly to the picture presented by the latest British work, as a basis for a speculative commentary on some of the possible effects of the new biology on the population development of the future.

It must be a matter of opinion whether the new biology of today represents more than a continuance of a steady long-term trend line of research progress, and whether it stands clear above that line as an exceptional group of advances. However, if a similar question is asked about the population prospects, as presented in the official projections, there can be no doubt about the answer: each one in its turn is founded on the assumption of a continuity between the past and the future, which meet at the point of departure for each projection. Although the course of mortality, fertility and migration is studied for the purpose of making the projections, no attempt is made to separate out the influences on these elements of individual changes in the general environment, for example developments in the structure of society, in the economic situation, in the political scene or in science. In general, it is assumed that nothing exceptional is suddenly taking place, considering all these influences in combination; this being so, it may be said, without much danger of contradiction, that similarly no allowance is made for the emergence of an exceptional situation in any one separate influence; so, if there is today any abnormal new biology, its effects do not emerge in the projections. Thus there is room for me to hypothecate, for your entertainment, some really startling biological influences and to discuss the special new effects they might have on the future population. I do not want to attempt too involved an analysis, which would result if I were to tackle social, economic or other non-biological influences as well; but in so far as it seems likely that they would operate to mitigate, or to reinforce, biological effects, some reference must be made to them.

Given any complete set of assumed future rates of mortality, fertility and migration, classified by sex, age and year of expected occurrence, the present population can be projected with great speed for any distance ahead by means of computer programmes which are already in existence. There is no difficulty about this; any problems that arise are connected with the translation of the supposed normal biological influences into the corresponding changes in the demographic rates, particularly as regards the timing of the emergence of the effects. As a broad guide, making use of the conclusions I have drawn from the experience of the past hundred years, I have tried to apply the following principles in approaching these problems.

(a) By and large, the new biology which will affect the trend of population between now and the end of the century is that of the past three decades, and not that which is to emerge in the coming years.

(b) Moderate changes are more likely than extreme ones, because of public resistance, in some degree, or because of unforeseen setbacks.

(c) A yardstick of commonsense must be applied in the measurement of the outcome.

(d) British figures seem to provide for the purpose as adequate a measure as those for any other economically developed country, and it is in the Western world that the most immediate effects are likely to be observed.

The first of these principles leads me to exclude from consideration here such possible developments as the creation of human life outside the human body or the bringing to birth of an embryo in the laboratory—even though they are said to have been foreseen by Diderot, and even though some successful work on these ideas has recently been carried out. I similarly exclude direct gene-manipulation, or alteration of the sex of the foetus; I do not discuss an increase in the maximum life span to over 100 years, or the prospects of revivification from deep-freeze. Possibilities I do consider it less rash to contemplate are, in increasing order of speculativeness:

(i) the putting into practice of still more efficient methods of birth control;

(ii) the coupling of prognostication of the sex of the child before its birth with the aid of new abortion techniques, thus providing indirect human control over the sex-ratio;

(iii) further progress in preventing deaths from circulatory impairments and from cancer.

There is little new that I can say which has not already been said about the demographic effects of more efficient contraception and abortion. The average family size of the young British married couple of today is only about $2\frac{1}{4}$ children, and this must reflect people's intentions fairly closely. It is common knowledge that two children are needed for replacement, with a small margin against losses, and it seems unlikely that the average will stay appreciably below this in the long run, because personal and national aspirations are broadly in accord. Discussion must centre mainly on the elimination of "unwanted" children, and it has recently been persuasively argued that such an elimination is just what the new biology should enable us to achieve, thus making any positive Government population policy unnecessary. Clearly, however, children do not fall simply into the two categories: wanted and unwanted; they are desired in varying degree. It seems a remote chance that the population will achieve an exact rate of replacement, and hold this steady over a long period. For the sake of illustration, however, what it is convenient to have at this moment is an alternative population projection based on replacement fertility, coming into play almost immediately and persisting until the year 2000.

Given easy control over the sex-ratio at birth, what might one expect the British people to want to achieve? Surely, a fair balance of the sexes. Indeed, a strict application of the principle associated with the Bill to prevent discrimination against women would seem to require that the numbers of male and female infants should be compulsorily rendered equal! The most humane form of sex-balance would, however, be one in which the numbers of young men and women were evenly matched at the ages at which people most desire to marry. To illustrate how this might be achieved, I have had a projection made with an altered sex-ratio at birth, operating from 1973 onwards, which reduces the surplus of young males. It is difficult to achieve a perfect result because changes in the pattern of immigration and emigration in the future can cause a distortion, quite apart from developments in marriage habits which it seems impossible to forecast.

A steady reduction in mortality in the future is already assumed in the official population projections (see Fig. 6) and the effects of this on the population can be seen by comparing the results with that of a

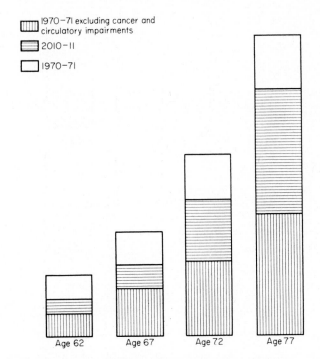

1970−71 excluding cancer and
circulatory impairments

2010−11

1970−71

Age 62   Age 67   Age 72   Age 77

FIG. 6. Mortality rates of women aged over 60, England and Wales (*a*) in 1970–71, (*b*) as projected to 2010–11, (*c*) excluding cancer and circulatory impairments.

projection assuming that the death rate at each age remains in future at its present level. What one needs to know in addition, perhaps, is the extent of the effect that would be created if the research of recent years into the real reasons for death from cancer and circulatory impairments finally bore fruit so well as to eliminate these causes altogether. I feel that this effect is worth studying even though both Meade and Burch have argued in this volume that such a development is unlikely, and though its study might fall outside the application of the principles on which I have based this part of the lecture.

Figure 7 gives an indication of the size of the British population in 1970 and its expected size in the year 2000 according to the latest official projection. It also shows how far the prospect changes if it is assumed that fertility falls at once to replacement level and then stays there until the end of the century. Pressure would be released by some 4 per cent, which means $2\frac{1}{2}$ million people, on the reduced fertility basis. Growth above present numbers will, however, be 4 million, or about 8 per cent, in any event; this arises from the structure of the

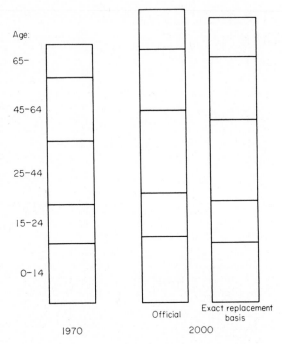

FIG. 7. Population, 1970 and projected population, 2000, Britain (millions).

population, which depends in turn on all the multifarious changes that have occurred since the beginning of the century.

The age-analysis included demonstrates the working of such structural changes; the 21 million people aged 0–25 today moving, in 30 years' time, mostly into the 25–44 age group and raising the numbers there from 13 to 16½ million. On the lower fertility basis, this is the only material development. An increase from 7 to 8 million in the numbers over pension age would be partially offset, so far as dependency on the working population generally is concerned, by a fall in the number of children under 15. But on the basis of a material proportion of families exceeding two children, as at present, the number of young dependants would rise by 2 millions as well.

The disparity between 58 million and 60½ million is not a large one, but many people would, I feel, regard the smaller population as the preferable one. Strong support for its merits is provided by the prospects for the first half of the twenty-first century, while some further natural growth must be expected on either basis in that period, on the exact-replacement basis it would be relatively slight (perhaps 2 million) whereas on the higher basis it would be considerable (perhaps 10 million). The difference in total numbers on the two bases by the year 2050 represents about a 15 per cent margin, and this is indeed substantial.

Associated changes in migration trends could well offset this result, but I would not care to predict in which direction. Much might depend on the relative population pressure inside and outside the country, and this in turn involves comparisons of prospects with Europe and the Commonwealth, which I shall not attempt here.

A broad indication of the numbers of young men and young women in the country today is given in Fig. 8. There is an appreciable surplus of men as compared with women of the same age. The diagram shows also the prospective position at the end of the century as envisaged by the latest available official projection. The excess will then, it is expected, be proportionally much the same. Evidently it would be

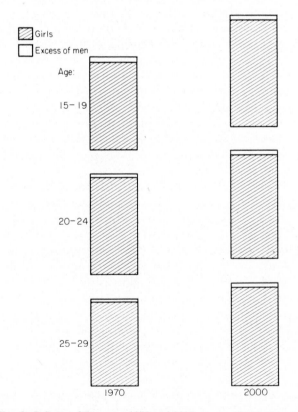

Fig. 8. Balance of the sexes, 1970 and 2000, at ages 15–30, Britain.

possible, given the means to which I have referred of controlling the relative numbers of births of each sex, to reduce the present bias in favour of boys, with the humanitarian intent of providing a general equality of mating opportunities. Less than a 5 per cent reduction in the frequency of male births would be required, and this is something which seems capable of being achieved spontaneously by the actions of a dedicated minority, without the need for any change at all on the part of most people—unless of course it is counteracted by new tendencies to favour males, such as are experienced in some developing countries.

This is the sort of idea which might have appealed to an H. G. Wells, or even more, perhaps, to a George Bernard Shaw. But having put it before you, I feel I must confess that, so far as I can see, there are a number of reasons why it seems most unlikely that any permanent exact balance could be relied upon in advance. First, men do not, on average, marry women of the same age but somewhat younger women. This has always been so, though the trend towards sex-equality might eventually eliminate it. The difference in marriage age helps to balance up the numbers of people at marriageable age, for the ratio of the numbers of men aged (say) 20–34 to women aged (say) 15–29 at present is just under unity; and in the year 2000 it will be only just over unity. My researches into the British statistics of the past, and on an international scale, have shown that the relative age-distributions of marrying couples adapt themselves freely to the local supply and demand situation—so much so that one cannot discern clearly what is the underlying biological pattern of age-preferences. Secondly, there is so much scope today for divorce and remarriage, and for partnerships outside marriage, that an imbalance can hardly be considered as providing an insuperable obstacle to gratification. Thirdly, migration is a potent factor, affecting the relative numbers of young men and women particularly, and one which is very hard to forecast. Finally, other social and economic influences are potent in relation to marriage, and these too are largely unforeseeable.

In Fig. 9, the numbers and age-distribution of older people in Britain in 1970 are indicated. About $8\frac{1}{2}$ million are over the national insurance pension ages of 65 for men and 60 for women, and this represents about 16 per cent of the total at all ages. According to the official projection, the corresponding number of potential pensioners will be nearly $9\frac{1}{4}$ million, again about 16 per cent of the total population. If mortality did not improve at all, however, and remained at its current level at all ages, there would be only 9 million of pension age—15 per cent not 16 per cent. This would bring such

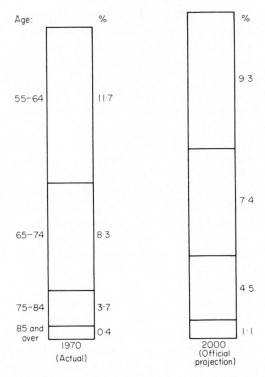

Age: %   %

                                                     9·3

55–64   11·7

                                                     7·4

65–74   8·3

                                                     4·5

75–84   3·7
85 and   0·4   1·1
over   1970   2000
           (Actual)   (Official
                                        projection)

Fig. 9. Numbers and proportions of people aged 55 and over Britain, 1970 and 2000.

benefits as a reduction of population pressure generally, relief of the contributions and taxes which are collected for the support of the aged and the sick, and a more youthful outlook, on the average, on affairs of the day. Capital wealth would be shared out more speedily through inheritance and death duties. The expectation of life at birth would be 72 rather than 73 (for the sexes combined) and that at age 60 would be 16 rather than 17, which on the face of it does not seem a big deprivation of living-power. Yet the gain in welfare, in individual cases, from improved survival chances would be rated, by most people, as the over-riding consideration.

An assumption of an exceptional new biological development clearly requires some further prolongation of life than that so far described. But this can hardly be said to stem from the medical advances of the past decade or two. Although at least one form of cancer is now curable, and survival rates of established sufferers have been improved, and although there are new treatments for circulatory impairments, the elimination of all deaths from these causes seems very unlikely as a consequence for the immediate future. The proportion of all mortality at the older ages which is attributable to these causes was shown in Fig. 6, which also indicated the extent of improvement envisaged by the official population projections. A suitable basis for my approach to this part of the lecture would perhaps lie somewhere in between the two. For the sake purely of illustration, however, I shall give the results of a complete elimination of deaths from cancer and heart diseases, as they are at present classified; then the effects of many improvements of a less radical character can be seen quite readily by the use of inter-polation. The exercise is clearly a notional one, for it must be suspected that multiple causes of death are often at work towards the end of life, and it must be a gross over-simplification to proceed in this manner: either the incidence of some of the other causes would be reduced as a consequence, or death would occur soon for some other reason.

Nevertheless, for what they are worth, I have used the much lighter residual death rates from Fig. 6. If they came into operation today, the population of pension age or over in the year 2000 would be as high as 15 million, 23 per cent of the grand total at all ages of 66 million. If we were forecasting for that year, no doubt a more realistic "high" assumption would lead to say 11 million old people, or an 18 per cent slice of the population. But the way towards the higher proportion by (say) 2025 or 2050 would be paved. These figures give food for thought for those who are concerned with the implications, or potential impli-cations, of the new biology. One certainly feels that public reaction might do much to prevent its effective use in this particular case.

Nevertheless, to sum up, the likely influences of the new biology on the population developments of the next thirty years, taking all my three examples together, are not very radical. They need not affect the total much, if gains in longevity are offset by reduced fertility. The balance of the sexes could be improved a little. An older age-distribution seems the only really likely outcome. But any deleterious effects from this could easily be offset if medical advances permit the retention of health, vigour and a youthful outlook for a year or two longer than at present. It is still possible for the quality of life to be improved generally, on the basis of general social and economic progress.

References

Banks, J. A. (1954). *Prosperity and Parenthood*. London: Routledge and Kegan Paul.
Brech, R. (1963). *Britain, 1984*. London: Darton, Longman and Todd.
Brewer, T. H. (1971). Disease and social class. In *The Social Responsibility of the Scientist*. Edited by Martin Brown. London: Collier-Macmillan.

Bourgeois-Pichat, J. (1972). In 200 years so many things can happen. *Population Index*, **38,** 306.

Burkitt, D. P. (1973). Some diseases characteristic of modern Western civilization. *Br. med. J.*, **1,** 274–278.

Charles, J. (1964). In *The World in 1984*. London: Penguin, New Scientist Series.

Gurdon, J. B. (1968). Transplanted nuclei and cell differentiation. *Scient. Am.*, December.

McKeown, T. (1965). Medicine and world population. In *Public Health and Population Change*. University of Pittsburgh Press.

Meade, J. E. (1973). Economic policy and the threat of doom. In *Resources and Population*. London. Academic Press.

Peel, J. (1970). The Hull family survey. I. The survey couples, 1966. *J. biosoc. Sci.*, **2,** 45–70.

Peel, J. (1972). The Hull family survey. II. Family planning in the first 5 years of marriage. *J. biosoc. Sci.*, **4,** 333–346.

Starke, L. G. K. (1952). Time-changes in the mortality rate: an experimental formula. *J. Inst. Actuaries*, **78,** 192.

Taylor, G. R. (1968). *The Biological Time Bomb*. London: Thames and Hudson.

The Economist's Approach to the Doctor's Dilemma

Department of Health and Social Security, London, England

The views expressed in this paper are the views of the author and should not be taken to represent the views of the Department of Health and Social Security.

The early chapters of André Maurois' (1959) biography of Alexander Fleming are enlivened by the personality of Fleming's teacher, Sir Almroth Wright. One evening in the early years of the century, while Bernard Shaw was drinking tea in Wright's laboratory at St Mary's Hospital, the question arose of whether a new patient should be admitted. Shaw asked what would happen if more people needed help than could properly be looked after, and Wright replied: "We should have to consider which life was best worth saving." This is the theme of Shaw's play *The Doctor's Dilemma*, which appeared in 1906.

It is a familiar fact that the discovery by Fleming of the antibacterial action of penicillin, as early as 1928, was not seriously followed up until the beginning of the war, but the requirements of the services then resulted in the technical problems of production being rapidly overcome by Florey, Chain and others. Later on in his biography of Fleming, Maurois explains that towards the end of the war the supply of penicillin had reached a level at which the military authorities were beginning to permit its selective use for civilian patients. Sometimes, says Maurois, the identity of the patient had an influence on the decision. He quotes only one example, that of a well-known literary figure of the time, a biographer of Winston Churchill. Unfortunately the patient died, like Louis Dubedat in Shaw's play.

The choice of which life to save when two or more patients claim the same drug, or piece of equipment, or doctor's time, is a moral one and the contribution which economics can make to such decisions is an indirect one, even if it exists. These decisions are taken by the particular doctor concerned in the clinical situation prevailing. It is hardly an obligation which doctors can be presumed to enjoy, but they are unlikely to brook much interference from economists in their disagreeable task.

Of course, economics is involved, because doctors can only do their best with the facilities they are given; what they are given is certain to determine to a greater or lesser extent what kind of work they can do, and what kind of patients they can treat. It sets the framework within which disagreeable choices may arise. Even outside the clinical situation, where it is a matter of what facilities to provide rather than how and on whom they should be used, the Department of Health usually confines itself to the rôle of dispenser of money and advice. The criticism has sometimes been levelled that it is a good deal freer with the latter than the former, so that regional and area authorities find themselves unable to do all they are advised to do, let alone all they would like to do. They are thus unable to escape the need for painful choices in determining what facilities to provide. In this respect, the Department is doing unto others as it is done by the Treasury. When some new and costly object of expenditure is invented by the researchers, the response of the Treasury is normally to invite the Department to reconsider its order of priorities to see whether it wishes to displace any of its existing programmes in favour of the new invention. This is the only practical way to do it. It is always difficult, and often impossible, to drop existing programmes or even cut them down. Again thanks to antibiotics, the National Health Service was able to live off the carcass of the TB services for many years, but this was an unusual bonus. But the total of public expenditure is so vast, and the range of programmes covered is so extensive and disparate, that it would be quite impossible to reappraise priorities right across the board at frequent intervals.

In the nature of the case, specific scarcities of medical resources are likely to arise where techniques have been newly developed, and are still to some extent experimental. In such cases it is often justifiable, and always to some degree plausible, to restrict access to the new mode of treatment on grounds of its unproven efficacy, the possibility of adverse side-effects and so forth, rather than on economic grounds. It is very difficult for a layman to sort out the genuine from the specious here. As a matter of fact, a great many medical treatments involve an element of risk. It appears that so-called iatrogenic disease (disease induced by medical care itself) accounts for as much as 5 per cent of all acute medical admissions (Miller, 1973). In the case of any treatment there may be a range of possible outcomes, some good, some bad and some indifferent. To each of these outcomes a probability can be attached, and a decision to undertake (or to submit to) the treatment formally requires a valuation of these various outcomes, and weighting each by its probability. If the weighted sum of the good outcomes exceeds the weighted sum of the bad outcomes, reason indicates that the treatment should be undertaken. But there is nothing in this about costs. Surely, before one undertakes a treatment costing, say £10,000, one would like to know that the weighted sum of the outcomes amounts to £10,000 worth of benefit. That is to say, it should not be enough that the treatment should be expected to do *some* good. The expected benefit should be expected to exceed the cost.

Perhaps the right of doctors to choose how and on whom to use the facilities that are provided by the NHS is not an absolute one. Without question, the responsibility of the doctor to the patient in his care is of the greatest moment. A system of health care could hardly be tolerable in which this responsibility was seriously qualified. Apart from anything else, it is important to the patient's recovery that he should think the doctor is unequivocally on his side and doing his best. But in using the resources provided, the doctor also has a responsibility to society at large, which society has conceded, no doubt wisely, to the doctors as a profession; and it is not suggested that this responsibility is not handsomely fulfilled.

But there is a potential conflict between the obligation of the doctor to the individual patient and his obligation to society at large, and the doctor's dilemma in this extended sense has become much more pervasive since Fleming discovered penicillin.

The circumstances in which precious supplies of penicillin were available only to a favoured few did not last long. The inevitable progress of technology soon took the matter in hand, and the new drug was saving not only patients' lives but doctors' time and public money. But the sort of discovery which, like penicillin, not only prevents the deaths of large numbers of young adults but restores them to normal health and activity is a rarity—perhaps even a thing of the past. It is a familiar fact that the pattern of disease has been changed radically, largely by antibiotics, and that by preventing people dying quickly and generally cheaply doctors have not enabled them to live in perfect health for ever but only to die more slowly and often more expensively. A hundred years ago the number of therapies of proven effectiveness was so small that providing medical care to the best known standards could not have constituted a serious economic problem for society as a whole, though it clearly could be such for particular individuals. Even fifty years ago, when Fleming was about to make his discovery, the same could almost be said. Now we know we have a problem, and the question is whether it will continue to become more serious as medical science progresses. So far as one can see, we may have to come to terms with the fact that treatable conditions of a non-trivial kind may increasingly have to be treated by other than the technically optimal methods for economic reasons. That is to say, society may have to decide whether it wishes to divert increasingly large proportions of the social product into health care, or whether it would rather do something else with the money. It is not obvious that this particular situation is going to arise. After all, we are getting richer all the time, and not all the discoveries of medical science are of a cost-increasing kind. But historically the share of the national product going to health care, and the share which can be justified in terms of its effectiveness as doing so, has increased, and presumably it has to stop somewhere.

There have been some special problems. To some extent the economic aspect has been brought to light, (one could hardly say "exacerbated"), by the socialization of medical care through the NHS. This must surely have given access to care to many who were previously inadequately provided for. Demographic pressure on the service has been intensified because those millions of babies who were born around the turn of the century are now making their presence felt as they become increasingly infirm. However, it is already clear, and has been the subject of frequent comment, that resources for health care are short, and this means that people must sometimes be treated by methods which are technically less than the absolute best. In fact it is almost certainly a condition of the efficient running of the economy that it should be so. If all patients, whatever they were suffering from, were treated in the most lavish and sophisticated fashion, it would certainly mean that the educational service or some other public service was getting less than its share.

This is the essential issue of priorities in medicine. Situations in which no treatment at all is given, or inadequate treatment, because of specific shortage of resources should be, and surely are, rather rare.

The problem is not particular to Britain, though it shows itself in different forms. In no advanced country, one may hazard, does pure fee-for-service still prevail. Largely because the possible fees are so colossal, insurance is very general. But in a private insurance system, although there may be a substantial element of what the Americans call "co-insurance", i.e. the patient has to pay a percentage, the cost at the time of need is, by definition, a subsidized one, and what is more there are no constraints on the total budget such as one finds in the NHS Thus treatment costs and premiums continue to rise, and it is a current subject of anguished debate in the United States how insurance can be extended to cover those needy and under-privileged groups who are still left out without an unacceptable increase in total costs. A recent US estimate (Feldstein, 1973) put the economic waste caused by over-utilization of insured medical care at upwards of $4 thousand million a year and perhaps as high as $9 thousand million— nearly twice the cost of the NHS.

Economists have operated mainly on the level of these larger questions. The prime interest of the discussion by economists of the value of life has been to try to determine how large a budget should be devoted to life-saving activities, either in general or of specific kinds, such as kidney machines or road improvements, rather than to value the lives of particular individuals as in *The Doctor's Dilemma*. But of course the principles one adopts in valuing lives generally can be applied to individuals.

If one derives an average or typical value of life from values of individual lives, then the average or typical value can have no greater validity than the individual values. Of course, the average values so derived may be qualified in various ways, but this seems to me merely to cast doubt on the basic method of valuation. Economists have been discussing the value of life for a long time, at least since the middle of the seventeenth century. Sir William Petty is usually regarded as the first serious exponent of this particular form of political arithmetic (Hull, 1899), and his method has stood the test of time, though whether it stands the tests of logic and commonsense is another matter.

Petty and his followers took, by implication, a rather low view of humanity in this context, valuing it much as one would value a slave, i.e. in terms of what he can produce; but it is fair to say that although the rôle of the patients in these analyses has servile implications, the motives which led economists to impute this rôle to them were liberal enough. What they were saying was that, if it would be worthwhile to save the life of a slave in such circumstances, how much more worthwhile must it not be to save a fellow citizen. The latest published Road Research Laboratory figures (Dawson, 1971) value the life of the average fatal motor accident victim at £12,000 on this basis. One can still get quite a lot of medical care for £12,000—six months in the most expensive intensive care unit, for example.

In valuing a slave, one has to take into account the fact that he eats, and consumes things generally. It is therefore only the value of his net output which should come into the reckoning. This might at first appear to be a serious objection to this method of valuing the lives of free men, who are observed to consume pretty freely without the inhibiting influence of a slave-master. But rates of taxation, direct and indirect, have now reached levels at which a good many people are, as they say, working more for the government than for themselves. One might say that the public at large has close to a half share in the equity of the average working man. And of course it is not just a question of the public at large. Most wage and salary earners have dependants, so that the share of each earner's earnings which is literally self-consumed may be quite small. We all have a very considerable interest in keeping each other alive and working.

But few people nowadays go on working until they drop, so in saving the life of today's worker society is incurring a moral, and even a legal, obligation to keep him in modest comfort or possibly modest discomfort for the rest of his life. In fact the Department recently published some calculations (Department of Health and Social Security, 1972) of the effects on public expenditure on health and social security of the changes in morbidity and mortality which would result from certain postulated reductions in cigarette smoking, and the conclusion reached was that by the end of the century the additional costs incurred by people keeping alive would exceed the costs saved. The cost of living exceeds the cost of dying. One need not conclude from this that cigarette smoking is something the Department would wish to encourage, as a means of reducing its commitment to the care of the elderly.

There is a sense in which the present value—i.e. the future annual values discounted at the appropriate of discount, whatever that may be—of a person's output, net of his consumption, represents the irreducible minimum value he has to society. As such, this measure is very useful so long as one is confident that the value so derived exceeds the cost of treatment, and so long as one is in favour of more treatment. But the very fact that the producers and earners among us are called upon to contribute so heavily, not only to the general overheads of society, but to the maintenance of the non-producers and non-earners, the low-producers and low-earners, itself implies that the value society puts on people is only very imperfectly represented by the capacity to produce and earn. Twenty years ago the terms Welfare State and National Health Service were virtual synonyms in common parlance. The principle of equal access to medical care which underlies the NHS commands very general popular acceptance, and this in itself seems to argue against the use of output as a measure of the value of life. The public would not stand for it.

If it is a question of some catastrophic disease, what determines the individual's ability to get access to treatment under a system of private medical care is not his income but his wealth, and this is even more unequally distributed than income. Egalitarian sentiment apart, may not the willingness of a person to use his wealth to preserve his life also affect one's view of his value? What would one think of an ancient wealthy valetudinarian who was willing to impoverish his dependants in order to buy a brief extension of his existence? Might he not be thought, and not least by his dependants, to have less moral worth than another who was prepared to do a little self-sacrifice in such circumstances?

Producing mature human beings is quite an expensive affair, and a second line of thought on valuing people, also traceable to Petty, is to measure their cost of production, presumably accumulated to the present at a suitable rate of interest, but allowing as far as possible for depreciation. In fact the rate of investment in human capital in terms of the cost of rearing children, the educational system, training and health services is now comparable in scale with investment in industrial and commercial capital. It can be calculated that the present value, discounted at 10 per cent, of the public sector cost of raising the average child to maturity was very roughly £2,000 in 1970, and that the average net cost to the parents, similarly discounted, of a marginal child in the family was about £700.

There seem to be two possible lines of argument in favour of this method of valuation but neither carries conviction. The first is that having spent large sums on rearing people it is wasteful to let them die. The second is that whoever made the investment in the first place must have thought it worth while.

On the whole, such methods of valuation, although they have a long history are now becoming rather unfashionable among economists, who are sometimes a little embarrassed by the enthusiasm of others for their use. They lack any clear logical foundation in the context of a free society, and their anti-egalitarian implications are against the spirit of the times, and bear particularly adversely on those elderly and otherwise incapacitated members of society who are now the main source of demand for medical care.

The outcome of medical care, or no care, or of the various other events which can kill or preserve us is a matter of probabilities, rather than certainties. Similarly, many of the decisions which an individual takes in the course of his ordinary existence, such as the decision whether to go to work on the bus or on a bicycle may denote very small absolute variations in the probability of survival, and in some cases, such as the bus vs. cycle case, they also involve variations in cost. Realistically, there is some sense in studying people's reactions to differences in the probabilities of death which are associated with differences in cost (Schelling, 1968). It is also claimed that people are likely to be able to form opinions about changes in these small probabilities more calmly and more rationally than they can contemplate the awful question of how much it is worth to them to be alive rather than dead. If for the sake of simplicity, we assume that a million people each have a one-in-one hundred thousand chance of dying if a certain course of action is pursued, e.g. going to work on a bicycle, but that this chance is reduced by half if some other course is pursued, e.g. going on the bus, we may be able to elicit the money value they would each place on this improvement in their own prospects, either by observing actual patterns of behaviour or by special experiments; and by aggregating these values we could estimate the average value of each life expected to be saved.

This approach rests on stronger logical foundations than the ones criticized above. It is an attempt at valuing life itself, rather than valuing something quite different. But some difficulties remain.

First, people are notoriously irrational in their behaviour in face of risk, as the statistics on insurance show. It may be possible by experimental means to overcome this difficulty to some extent. But to this extent one is in fact demanding that the individual should form a consciously rational judgment of the matter, which must still consist of a combination of two elements: the perception of the probability, or rather the change in probabilities, and the valuation of life itself. It may be that there are psychological advantages in a somewhat devious probabilistic approach to the matter but the need for a judgment of the value of life itself seems to be inescapable if a rational conclusion is to be reached.

In a sense, any answer will do if all we want to know is how the unreflecting person assesses the risk of death; but are we trying to give people what they superficially seem to want, or are we trying to give them what they would want if they were rational about it? There may be no answer to the latter question, but it may be the one we ought to be asking.

In the context of the relative valuation of different people's lives, it is relevant that this form of analysis depends on subjective assessment by the individuals concerned. We should hardly be willing to accept these valuations as the means of resolving the doctor's dilemma. By doing so we should be committed to saving the timid, the self-important and those who lacked the comforts of religion; and, among the religious, those who had most reason to postpone a confrontation with their Maker.

This does not exhaust the methods which economists have employed or proposed to employ for valuing life but it is perhaps sufficient for illustration. In general, they are not properly articulated with the aspirations and objectives of social concern and public policy.

In fact they answer the wrong questions. This is not to deny that it matters what criterion one adopts. J. L. Roberts, in an unpublished study of accidents in the home, has attempted to estimate the relative shares of the losses which are attributed to various age groups, in order to identify important target groups for educational activities. For example, taking fatal accidents only, persons aged 65 and over constitute 12 per cent of the population, but account for 64 per cent of deaths resulting from home accidents. The Road Research Laboratory's method would attribute only 7 per cent of the total loss to that group, because of their low earning capacity. In terms of life-years lost, the share of the over 65s is 21 per cent; but if life-years lost are discounted at 5 per cent, on the grounds that a life-year saved next year is worth more than one saved in fifty years time, the percentage of total loss attributable to the group rises to 38 per cent, and at 10 per cent discount it becomes 47 per cent, because the elderly do not have to wait so long, on the average, to enjoy their remaining years of life. Thus on different criteria, none conspicuously more or less defensible than the rest, one can get the following answers to the question: What share of the loss from fatal home accidents falls on the over 65s?—7 per cent; 21 per cent; 64 per cent; 38 per cent and 47 per cent. In all, Roberts has tried nineteen methods of valuation, and arrives at a set of figures which contain a member of every decile group except the two highest.

The judgments required are moral rather than economic. There would be a good deal of agreement, e.g. that no distinction should be made for the usual list of reasons—sex, race, and social class, but that the value of survival was positively related to expectation of life and to the quality of the life to be expected.

At a cost of £5,000, a treatment which would give someone twenty more years of good quality life would seem to many to be a bargain. At £500,000 it might not. At £50,000 one might not be sure, but would any amount of esoteric economic calculation help one make up one's mind? The quality of death also seems to be important: how much is it being dead that matters, and how much how one becomes dead? But this introduces broader issues.

There is a second aspect of Roberts' study which is rather significant. The number of injuries of different severities is inversely proportional to the severity of the injury. Minor injuries outnumbered severe injuries by about 10 to 1, and severe injuries outnumbered fatal injuries also by about 10 to 1. Thus it becomes very important what relative weight one gives to the various degrees of severity in measuring the total effect of accidents.

Rather a small part of the work of the NHS is concerned with saving people's lives, or failing to do so. A great deal of time and money goes into treating conditions which, though acute, are not dangerous to life, and still more which are chronic. The major economic issues which confront the Service and the Department concern the balance which should be struck between life-saving activities, and treatment of acute conditions in general, and care of those suffering from chronic diseases and disabilities.

In economics, value denotes exchange value. The exchange may be actual or potential, and of course in any situation a variety of exchanges may be possible. What is the most relevant exchange—what are we most clearly giving up when we undertake a heart-transplant, or put someone on a kidney machine, or into a bed in a neurosurgical unit?

Not, probably, 0·0001 per cent off the rate of VAT, or two soldiers in Germany, or half a primary school classroom. It is more likely to be a few hundred home nurse visits, or a renovated ward for the mentally handicapped, or a few dozen hernia operations. To an economist, the great thing about the NHS, especially the reorganized NHS, is that it makes us face these choices, and offers a framework for doing so. There is a specific health budget to be allocated. In recent years there has been much more emphasis on the less dramatic forms of activity, and a little has been done, as it is thought, to redress the balance between the acute and the previously under-privileged chronic case. There is also a good deal of interest among economists and statisticians, both in this country and abroad, in devising measures which could be capable of relating the values, not necessarily in money terms, of different kinds of medical care whether involving the prevention of death, the relief of pain and disability etc. These indices are as yet barely in the experimental stage (Symposium on the Measurement of Ill Health, 1972 and 1973), but in principle they offer a way of formalizing the relationship between the various kinds of benefits we are trying to achieve, and they may some day help in guiding the rational deployment of resources at a strategic level. But there are limits.

In Shaw's play, the anti-hero, Louis Dubedat, dies. Sir Colenso Ridgeon connives at his being killed by the incompetence of a distinguished colleague to whom he disingenuously entrusts the application of the precious vaccine. Ridgeon's reasons for doing so are complex, but one can distinguish four: (1) a moral preference for saving a hardworking and impecunious colleague, (2) detestation of Dubedat's moral character, (3) a wish to protect Dubedat's wife from an eventual recognition that her husband is a scoundrel, and (4) a desire to acquire the lady for himself.

None of these relates at all directly to the capacity of Dubedat as a producer or earner, though in fact his capacities as producer would probably need to be distinguished rather carefully from those as an earner, he being an artist whose genius is as yet unrecognized. In fact it seems to be the third and fourth reasons which sway Ridgeon. When it comes to putting a value on human life the economist feels constrained to agree with Shaw's competitor in the dramaturgical stakes that "There are more things in heaven and earth, Horatio, than are dreamt of in your philosophy".

References

Dawson, R. F. F. (1971). *Current Cost of Road Accidents in Great Britain*. Road Research Laboratory, Report LR 396. London: H.M.S.O.

Department of Health and Social Security. (1972). *Smoking and Health. A study of the effects of a reduction in cigarette smoking on mortality and morbidity rates, on health care and social security expenditure and on productive potential*. London.

Feldstein, M. S. (1973). The welfare loss of excess health insurance. *Journal of Political Economy*, **81**, 2, 1, 251.

Hull, C. H. (Ed.) (1899). *The Economic Writings of Sir William Petty*. London: Cambridge University Press.

Maurois, A. (1959). *Life of Sir Alexander Fleming*. London: Cape.

Miller, H. (1973). *Medicine and Society*. London: Oxford University Press.

Schelling, T. C. (1968). The life you save may be your own. In *Problems in Public Expenditure Analysis*. Edited by S. B. Chase. Washington DC: Brookings.

Symposium on the Measurement of Ill Health. (1972, 1973). *International Journal of Epidemiology*, **1**, 4, and **2**, 1.

Legal Approaches to the New Biology

B. M. DICKENS

The College of Law, London, England

Introduction

An obvious feature of this symposium on Population and the New Biology has been its concern with the ways in which present, rather specialized, knowledge is likely to affect the future of the general community. I am afraid, however, that as a lawyer, I am at a disadvantage in considering the future. The law does, of course, prescribe rules which attempt to govern future events, but these rules tend at their best to be fashioned by the experiences and perceptions of the existing general community. Research in medical science leads to new achievements giving rise to new implications lying at first beyond the experience of those authorities in the community that condition the content of the law, and so we must not be surprised that these advances may expose the law as unprepared and inadequate. The law is inclined to lack specialized foresight in medical and biological matters.

The Judicial Basis of the Law

I want in this paper to consider primarily judicial rather than legis-lative attitudes, even though the law in this country comes to us from both sources; that is, from judicial reasoning in decided cases and from Acts legislated by Parliament. If you find that the judicial approaches I shall be discussing reveal an unrealistic or unhelpful understanding of affairs, you can influence the law, in the same way as for instance the Abortion Law Reform Association did, by urging new legislation. In our constitutional system the judges accept new Acts of Parliament as

Numbers in parentheses are legal references. The complete list of these references is at the end of the paper.

superseding established precedent and their own preferences. I hope, incidentally, that I am not being over defensive in pointing out that within our system of democratic law-making by Parliament, defective though it may be, lawyers do not bear sole responsibility for the condition of the law.

The distinction drawn between judge-made law on the one hand and Parliamentary law on the other is not absolute. An Act of Parliament still has to be interpreted by judges before its true legal meaning is known. We are therefore very much influenced in our understanding of the law by the attitudes shown by judges, whether to case precedents or to Acts of Parliament.

An important and distinctive feature of the English legal system is not simply that courts follow established judgments laid down by the higher courts, but that they are bound to follow such judgments; we have a system of binding precedent. We need not consider now the techniques of legal argument and judicial craftsmanship that enable a particular judge to favour one line of binding precedent over another apparently equally binding line of precedent, but we must pay regard to the powerful influence exerted by judges in the higher courts. Their underlying attitudes dominate the approach lawyers take when advising and acting upon particular issues, including novel issues which have not so far actually come before the courts. The point must be emphasized that lawyers apply by analogy to new questions the precedents laid down by the higher courts in relevant earlier judgments, because many of the issues raised by advances in biology have never been the subject of litigation. The courts do not try hypothetical questions, and judgments can therefore be given only when issues arise in the litigation of real cases. Where, as a matter of experience, cases do not arise before the courts, the judgments that define the law are obviously few, and the law tends to be indefinite. This condition is regressive, of course, because a good reason for not prosecuting a criminal charge and for not undertaking the financial risks of a civil action, especially against a respected and highly qualified medical practitioner, is that the law is uncertain.

In the face of uncertainty, the judges tend to react according to their traditional instincts, which are conservative, unsympathetic to innovation and the promotion of a new image of society and of social relationships. Judges automatically assume the virtue of the *status quo*, in the sense of the image they have of how the public interest is best served, and the burden of proving that his different image of the public advantage is to be preferred falls upon the litigant with the new vision. This is so whether the litigant himself initiates the action by seeking judicial protection for some newly-asserted right, such as a right of privacy, which English judges have traditionally denied as such, or whether he is a defendant claiming some new legal justification, such as a right of euthanasia when charged with murder. The best-known instance of a judge accepting a new way of looking at the law is perhaps the *Bourne* case [1], tried in 1938, in which abortion was held lawful when intended to preserve the mental health of a mother whose life was not endangered by her pregnancy.

Other instances of this nature could be cited, such as the persuasive Scottish decision in *Maclennan v. Maclennan* in 1958 [2], holding after long controversy that artificial insemination by donor does not constitute adultery, but these reforming cases are not frequent. Moreover, when they do occur they tend to be not the sudden inversion of established legal principles, but the culmination of a long judicial and academic process of questioning, re-appraising and eventually amending the way lawyers conceive of the law, to achieve by evolution what would be resisted if attempted by revolution. An American artificial insemination doctor has described the development with particular clarity; she wrote:

> Any change in custom or practice in this emotionally charged area has always elicited a response from established custom and law of horrified negation at first; then negation without horror, then slow and gradual curiosity, study, evaluation, and finally a very slow but steady acceptance. (Kleegman and Kaufman, 1966).

Legal reform in this country has been conducted in much the same evolutionary way as social reform, and this is not surprising when one considers the social situation of the judges in whose hands for the time being the destiny of the law lies. It is not an original observation that our senior judges have tended to come from a confined segment of society (Abel-Smith and Stevens, 1967). Recruitment to the legal profession is today perhaps more liberal than it ever has been, but it remains overwhelmingly middle-class. Further, eleven out of twelve practising lawyers are solicitors, debarred as such from appointment to higher judicial office, and successful barristers will only be considered for appointment to the High Court, rarely at an age lower than forty-five, if they conform to the internal expectations of the Bar, which are essentially upper-class in derivation. Not all barristers begin their careers from this social background, of course, but they are no less able than ambitious men in other fields to adopt the social characteristics of the group to which they aspire to belong. In the not too distant past it was acceptable that judges were active in conventional politics before appointment (Edwards, 1964; Jackson, 1972), but this is less usual now. It remains vital, however, that they be respected among their colleagues at the Bar not only for their legal skills but also for their standards of integrity and social decency, and the holding of unconventional views on such matters as politics, religion, society or even law would not and still will not be considered decent (or, as it is often revealingly put, "safe"). The advocacy of distinctive opinions falling outside the range of acceptable dissent from the orthodox will tell against the appointment to the Bench of even the most distinguished barrister.

Our higher judges are a remote body of privileged and usually propertied men who have achieved recognition in the genteel atmosphere of the Bar. They tend through their training and experience to be responsive to the authorized version of social interpretation and readily associate themselves with Establishment views. They accept a rôle of social leadership, evidenced perhaps by the knighthood inevitably conferred upon them when appointed to the High Court, and they must surely contemplate acquiring authority at the highest pinnacle of both social and judicial elevation, the House of Lords.

The judges fulfil their function of social leadership not by taking society upon new adventures in law, which might defy the precedent by which all but the House of Lords are bound, but by preserving established social attitudes, which tend in the short-term to be restrictive of change. They often seem to speak with the authentic voice of responsible and traditional society, and guard it against the hardly perceived but instinctively-feared consequences of recognizing a different form of social order.

This attitude can perhaps be illustrated by quoting from a judgment of the present Master of the Rolls, Lord Denning. It may be fair to suggest that he has built a notable reputation among laymen and many lawyers for embodying in his judgments the good sense of the law, yet in 1954 when the Court of Appeal had to consider whether a husband's voluntary sterilization constituted cruelty to his wife for purposes of the divorce law (as it then was), he said of the operation that,

> When it is done with the man's consent for a just cause, it is quite lawful, as, for instance, when it is done to prevent the transmission of an hereditary disease; but when it is done without just cause or excuse, it is unlawful, even though the man consents to it. Take a case where a sterilization operation is done so as to enable a man to have the pleasure of sexual intercourse without shouldering the responsibilities attaching to it. The operation is then plainly injurious to the public interest. It is

degrading to the man himself. It is injurious to his wife and to any woman whom he may marry, to say nothing of the way it opens to licentiousness. [3]

It should be said that the other two judges in the Court of Appeal, including the then Master of the Rolls, Lord Evershed, expressly dissociated themselves from this puritanical observation, and now academic authorities reject it almost but not completely out of hand. Nevertheless, the reasoning by which Lord Denning supported his conclusion in 1954 is typical of that which might be adopted today in facing legal problems created by developments in biology; he relied upon a nineteenth-century prosecution for prize-fighting [4] and a 1934 conviction for indecent assault committed by a man who, with her consent, caned a seventeen-year old girl for purposes of sexual gratification [5].

The fact is that the law, because of the poverty of its raw materials of applicable judgments and modern statutes, conceives of novel issues, raised by sophisticated medical techniques, in rather basic and primitive terms. It is normally only the patient's consent to an operation, for instance, that prevents it being a criminal battery by the surgeon, and possibly aggravated battery such as the law describes, in a phrase curiously inapposite when applied to therapeutic surgery, as battery with intent to do grievous bodily harm (Williams, 1958). Further, the patient may not in law be capable of consenting to the operation, because whether consent can validly be given to interference with a person's own comfort is a matter of public policy, as seen by the judges (Williams, 1962). The legal authorities for that proposition, incidentally, are the 1934 conviction for indecent assault despite consent, and a case of 1603 in which a healthy youth asked his friend to cut off his left hand so that he would be more appealing as a beggar [6] they were both convicted of unlawful maiming.

Legal Approaches to Biological Developments

GENERALLY

In approaching such matters as artificial insemination, test-tube reproduction, organ transplantation and mechanical prolongation of the human life span, the law finds itself rooted in a rather simple understanding of birth, natural human existence and death. The legal consequences that follow from definition of these conditions can be very complex, of course, for instance in civil law relating to such diverse matters as inheritance of property, the creation and termination of interests in land and trust funds upon defined family contingencies, liability to one spouse for treatment of the other, and liability for injuries felt after birth caused to a child before birth, whether by the use of force or drugs. On the criminal side of the law, problems arise of defining liability for homicide, abortion and child destruction, to say nothing of such relatively minor matters as registration of births and deaths. But in identifying when life has begun and when life has ended, the law tends towards a simplicity of approach that will appeal more to the uninvolved layman than to the biologist, the medical practitioner or particularly the surgeon. At the point where legal definitions and requirements interact with medical definitions and requirements, risks arise on the one hand of legal restraints upon beneficial medical research and practice, and on the other hand of medical disregard of the legal rights of patients, their conceived but as yet unborn children and those whose bodies upon their death can be of use to the living. Before considering legal aspects of some particular issues in biological development, we might perhaps in a few words attempt to achieve a bird's-eye view of the general terrain.

Biological advances of present legal significance fall mainly into three categories; that is, first, those intended to prevent birth, second those intended to assist birth, and finally those intended to prolong life. The category of preventing birth includes for instance certain developments in contraception, sterilization, the use of prostaglandins and abortion. Biological developments to assist birth raise questions on such issues as artificial insemination by husband and particularly by donor, test-tube pregnancy and incubator motherhood. Prolongation of life involves problems on the use of machines, organ transplantation and general spare-part surgery affecting live and dead human donors, animal donors and manufactured organs. There is a possible fourth category of improving the quality of new life by processes of genetic engineering, but this area is legally unexplored at present.

It is interesting to remember at this point that many biological processes quite recently developed are now so established as to give rise to no or, at the most, very few legal problems. We have emerged from the nineteenth century situation in which the communication of contraceptive information was judged obscene, and have progressed to the advanced position in which the healthy can voluntarily contribute even parts of their own bodies to aid the unhealthy. Blood-transfusion, skin-grafting from a donor and corneal grafting ring no alarm bells in the lawyer's mind. They fall naturally into a province of medicine which ranges from superficial cosmetic surgery to the most intricate brain surgery which, even when fully successful, considerably alters the patient's personality. All that the law requires in these areas is the consent of the patient, either express or implied, and good faith and adequate skill and care on the part of the medical team.

At the other extreme there are potential developments in biology that the lawyer has scarcely begun to consider. The area of genetic engineering, for instance, seems as if it ought to pose problems, but these have not so far been explored. Clearly, the prevention of genetically-transmitted defects in children raises no legal difficulties, but problems may arise from applying techniques to pre-select the sex of a child, or to breed for quality, giving to children, who would without interference be perfectly healthy, a superior physical or intellectual inheritance. On the negative side of genetic development, there have been proposals to obstruct the marriage or the procreation of couples whose children would inevitably or very probably suffer from severe physical or mental handicaps. The law here has an absolutely clear approach of rejecting these proposals, and will resist interference with the right of individuals to marry and have children, whatever the eugenic, social and moral objections to their procreation may be, provided that the parties have the mental capacity to consent to the marriage. It is assumed that if she is legally capable of consenting to marriage, the female can also consent to the conception of her husband's child, and in law these two issues in a marriage are not separated. Legal capacity to marry includes legal capacity to conceive, even though it was said in the House of Lords in 1948 that the procreation of children does not "appear to be a principal end of marriage as understood in Christendom" [7].

In order to illustrate in greater detail how the law regarding the natural processes of birth and death is affected by new developments in biology, four issues may be selected for examination; these are artificial insemination by donor, test-tube reproduction, organ transplantation and mechanical prolongation of life.

ARTIFICIAL INSEMINATION

Artificial insemination by a husband has recently raised legal points only regarding whether this alone amounts to consummation of the marriage; on a weighty balance of opinion it seems not to. A problem in prospect may be the status and rights of inheritance of a child born several years after his father's death by means of artificially inseminating his mother with the father's frozen semen preserved in a sperm bank (Leach, 1972). Few new problems would arise if an unmarried woman were to conceive by artificial insemination, but the participation of a donor in the birth of a child to another man's wife seems to raise several legal issues of significance. Let it be said at first that the practice of AID is almost certainly not criminal (Feversham, 1960). This proposition may be based on the characteristically negative legal reasoning that the historic common law never contemplated the possibility, so it is not a common law crime (assuming it is not a conspiracy to corrupt public morals), and the practice does not appear contrary to any statute (Bartholomew, 1958; Stevas, 1961).

On the civil consequences of AID there are few if any relevant English judgments, but mention has been made of the persuasive Scottish case of *Maclennan v. Maclennan* in 1958 holding that the practice does not constitute adultery in divorce law even when the husband does not consent. This judgment is notable, because when AID first came before courts of common law jurisdiction it seemed that judges were straining legal definitions in order to condemn participants in such a conception. In the case of *Orford v. Orford*, tried in 1921 in Ontario, the judge observed that,

> the essence of the offence of adultery consists not in the moral turpitude of the act of sexual intercourse, but in the voluntary surrender to another person of the reproductive powers or faculties of the guilty person; and any submission of those powers to the service or enjoyment of any person other than the husband or wife comes within the definition of adultery. [8]

This mediaeval scholastic reasoning might, of course, have led to the divorce of both the wife and the donor, even though they were most probably quite unknown to each other.

The purpose of this reasoning was to lead on to the conclusion that represents the present law, that a child resulting from AID is illegitimate. As the Canadian judge explained in 1921,

> Sexual intercourse is adulterous because in the case of the woman, it involves the possibility of introducing into the family of the husband a false strain of blood. Any act on the part of the wife which does that would therefore be adulterous. [9]

This principle would make A.I.D. adulterous even when the husband agrees to it, and conversely would make intercourse after hysterectomy or with full contraceptive protection not adulterous, and today the equation of AID with adultery seems to be rejected for purposes of the law of divorce.

Nevertheless, a child conceived in this way, even with the husband's consent, cannot be legitimate, since it would import as much "a false strain of blood" into the husband's family as if he had condoned adultery. While the law is still feudal in seeing a family as a male-dominated body of persons tied by genealogical or blood links rather than by social ties of human affection, it may offer a number of mitigations. First, if the husband is capable of intercourse and sub-fertile but not completely sterile, the law applies a strong presumption that the child is a legitimate child of the marriage (Bevan, 1973). This presumption may be rebutted by suitable evidence, but the blood-group and physical matching of the donor with the husband may make rebuttal very difficult, to say nothing of the medical practice of using where possible a mixture of the husband's and the donor's semen, so that the child may in fact be the husband's. A second legal possibility if the child cannot be the husband's is for the husband and wife to adopt the child. This will involve public registration they would perhaps prefer to avoid, especially since the donor has been selected to give the child every chance of appearing to be the husband's (subject to the donor being selected for his greater intelligence), but public registration is unavoidable since it is a criminal offence under section 4 of the Perjury Act 1911 not to register an illegitimate child as such.

The only two further points that need be made on this topic are, first, that the Family Law Reform Act 1969 has considerably reduced the distinction between legitimacy and illegitimacy regarding succession to property. The Act greatly emancipates the illegitimate child, although discrimination survives, for instance to prevent succession to a title and, more important, to prevent inheritance on the intestate death of any relative other than a parent. The second point is that in practice the donor will most probably not know the wife and will be required to sign a declaration of disclaimer regarding her child. Nevertheless the effectiveness of such a disclaimer has not been tested in the courts, and, subject to tracing and identification of the child, he may have the same rights, and may equally have the same obligations, as any other father of an illegitimate child.

AID has been considered only in the context of conscientious medical practice; the law is even less prepared for fringe practitioners of artificial insemination, whether medically qualified or not, and for donors selling their semen in the way the late Professor Titmuss described the sale of blood donations in the United States of America (Titmuss, 1971).

TEST-TUBE REPRODUCTION

The expression "test-tube reproduction" may arouse thoughts of Bokanovsky's Process envisaged by Aldous Huxley in *Brave New World*, but the fantasy of 1932 has become much less fanciful forty years later.

In 1969 at Cambridge an egg from a human ovary was fertilized with human sperm by test-tube means and began natural development. The use of test-tube fertilization to achieve a woman's successful pregnancy by her husband or indeed by a donor would be regarded in law as another technique of artificial insemination. But the possibilities range wider than that.

It is already a practice to implant animal embryos into host animals of the same or of another species (Leach, 1972) and although at present there are great obstacles to fertilizing a human egg outside a mother and producing an embryo and then successfully incubating it inside a host animal, these obstacles may be no greater than have already been overcome in comparable developments. It may be premature but not pointless therefore to consider legal issues raised by test-tube pregnancy and birth, using the expression "test-tube" symbolically, of course, to represent all that is entailed in fertilization and foetal growth outside the human donor of the egg.

First, we may dismiss at once the misconceived objection made by certain people hostile to the 1969 Cambridge experiment that, although the fertilization itself may not have been unlawful, termination of the experiment constituted illegal abortion. This proposition of law may be rejected upon the pedantic ground that the Offences Against the Person Act 1861 defines the offence in section 58 as committed by any person who acts with intent to procure the miscarriage of a woman. Clearly, the whole point of the 1969 experiment was that no woman had ever experienced conception, and therefore none could miscarry within the meaning of the section.

A genuine test-tube birth would pose initial problems of definition, since the present legal conditions necessary for live birth are that the child must be alive after complete extrusion from the body of the mother [10] and must have an existence independent of the mother [11]. It has never before had to be asked whether this means only the natural human mother for the purpose of establishing the point of time at which the child is considered to be born alive and to have acquired a legal personality. In themselves, however, the conditions are equally applicable to an animal incubating (or host) mother, although they would be much more difficult to apply to a purely mechanical device. The legality of using mechanical and animal means of procuring human live birth may be accepted, both on the negative reasoning that there is nothing in common law nor in statute against use of such means, and on positive analogy with clinical means of assisting the viability of a foetus either unborn within the mother or born but in a mechanical incubator.

Other legal problems are whose the child would be and from whom it would inherit. It has been seen that a child created by AID seems not to be treated as the donor's, nor that of the mother's husband if she is married. It is accepted that the child is hers, because of its natural growth within her. In the case of a test-tube child, however, the female donor would have no greater involvement with the child than the male donor. If, as seems most likely when the process is developed, the two donors are husband and wife, the position may be analogous to that of artificial insemination by the husband, but this apparent solution will not necessarily apply in the very situation which is most likely to be experienced first, in which the incubator of the child is not an animal nor a machine, but another woman. The human incubator mother might be a close relative of the family, perhaps acting under a similar impulse to that of a kidney donor, and then the possibility of a conflict of interests might be reduced. If, however, she were analogous to a foster mother her feelings of objectivity might change over the months of the pregnancy, and upon birth of the child she might feel she had at least as much claim to it as the donor of the egg. The point need not be pursued now, but there is a movement under consideration to give parents who foster or adopt a child improved rights over the child as against those of the natural and lawful mother. The unsatisfactory legal position in this area may serve as a forewarning of issues to be faced when a test-tube egg is placed in a human host mother.

There are two additional but minor points to mention before considering organ transplantation. First, a human host mother would seem to be subject to the existing abortion law regarding termination of pregnancy. The 1861 Act governs conduct by and towards a "woman being with child", but by an understandable oversight does not require the child to be her own. Second, complete human host motherhood may offer to the husband of an infertile wife what AID offers to the wife of a sterile husband, whose feminine need to experience motherhood is sympathetically recognized. The matter seems not to have been raised anywhere, perhaps because of the social history of the husband's condoned adultery with adoption of his child, but it may be right to consider putting the husband's need to experience fatherhood upon a more honourable and open basis, especially since with artificial insemination there need be no sexual dealings with the mother that might disturb his relationship with his wife. If contraceptive techniques reduce the supply of unwanted children available for adoption, this method of producing a child of the male partner of the marriage may become as respectable as the existing method of producing a child of the female partner by AID.

ORGAN TRANSPLANTATION

The topic of organ transplantation is attracting a growing legal literature (e.g. Meyers, 1970; Kennedy, 1969, 1973; Dworkin, 1970) but the legal position on several important issues remains inconclusive in the absence of relevant judgments, including statutory interpretations. It may be useful, however, to indicate the questions with which lawyers are concerned, and the legal groundrules that give rise to these questions. There are three centres of legal interest, namely first, the recipient of an organ, second the living donor and third the dead donor. There is no need now to discuss the use of animal donors of organs suitable for human transplantation, since this would clearly avoid the legal issues to be faced with human donors.

The patient receiving the transplant is governed by the general law on surgical operations, which can be shown in part to date back to a time when surgeons were little more than ambitious but potentially lethal barbers. The present position may be analysed by reference to four general tests (Dworkin, 1970). First, and least contentious, is that the operation must be performed by a person with appropriate medical skills, meaning principally appropriate to the nature of the surgery intended, but in cases of dire necessity conceivably meaning appropriate in all of the surrounding conditions in which the operation has to be conducted. Second, the patient must give a full, free and informed consent, which may be either expressed or implied. In law it may be only the fact of consent that prevents an operation from being a serious assault on the patient by the surgeon, unless he wishes to risk acting without consent and rely upon the difficult legal defence of necessity to save another's life. A patient may normally be assumed to give at least an implied consent to essential surgery, but a surgeon acting despite his protests to save the life of a patient determined that his days should end might be allowed this legal defence of necessity. The factual problems of ensuring that the consent of a captive, impressionable and possibly apprehensive patient is full, free and informed are wider than need be considered now.

The third test to be applied to an operation is whether it is for the patient's benefit. This may appear obvious, but it might seem to rule out purely experimental major surgery of no physically therapeutic value to the patient, and might in principle cast some doubt upon such operations as ritual circumcision and more extensive cosmetic surgery, which have psychologically rather than physically beneficial purposes. The final and closely related test is that there must be a lawful justification. An abortion operation, for instance, might meet the three tests of medical skill, genuine consent and the patient's physical advantage in avoiding the natural rigours of pregnancy, but still be unlawful. Ethical and social considerations interact in what lawyers describe rather vaguely as public policy to determine whether or not there is a lawful justification for an operation. We have seen Lord Denning's condemnation on public policy grounds in 1954 of the sterilization operation, and that today the legality of the operation is no longer in serious doubt. Equally, ritual circumcision and cosmetic surgery would probably be held lawful on public policy grounds of tolerance of moderate religious precepts and indulgence of personal vanity.

A further point to make regarding the transplant patient is that he has no right to demand the operation simply because it is surgically possible and a suitable donor is available. The decision on operating is purely medical, and the law will be very cautious indeed in seeming to interfere in questions of medical judgment and priority. The law is not concerned with itself taking correct medical decisions, but is concerned that medical decisions shall be correctly taken; that is, by the persons properly responsible for the patient and for the distribution of medical resources. As against this, a doctor responsible for a patient cannot lawfully refuse available and ordinary treatment on grounds of his own non-medical convictions, except under section 4(1) of the Abortion Act 1967, which provides for a doctor's conscientious objections to the operation. Nevertheless, as before this Act, he still risks liability for manslaughter by negligence and civil liability in addition in refusing to participate in an abortion upon proper indications [12].

Turning now to the live donor of the organ to be transplanted, we must realise that he is also a potential patient of surgery, and the four general tests we have just seen apply equally to him. The test of surgical skill needs no discussion, but the question of consent is of legal importance because, as was seen in the 1603 case of cutting off the beggar's hand, and the 1934 indecent assault case, even consent may not make physical harm lawful. A living person cannot donate his heart or liver, and we need consider only kidney transplants. The actual operation of kidney removal obviously involves infliction of bodily harm, but it causes no great disability in most cases to lose one kidney, because the other quickly undertakes all necessary functions within the donor. Consent can lawfully be given to transient or trifling harm, such as in a blood donation, or skin graft, but it is a matter of degree whether the harm of kidney removal can be so described because, apart from risks during the operation, any later infection or injury affecting the remaining kidney will clearly be of much greater significance to the donor. The genuineness of consent may also have to be questioned when the donor is under strong emotional pressures, especially if originating within the family of which he and the potential recipient are both members.

This aspect relates also to the third test of benefit to the patient, because kidney removal from a healthy person cannot be physically therapeutic as far as he is concerned. On the other hand it may be psychologically or emotionally beneficial to him to make the sacrifice, especially for a person dear to him, and in any event the law accommodates heroism. A person does not act unlawfully who runs into a burning house to rescue a trapped child, the law recognizing that "danger invites rescue", and by analogy an individual may similarly be able to put himself at reasonable risk to save the life of another. This reasoning would seem to satisfy the fourth test by providing a lawful justification for operating upon a healthy person, and vindicate the legality of existing practice, but in the absence of a favourable judicial decision or legislation some margin of doubt must remain.

This is not to suggest, however, that legislation will in itself remove legal difficulties, since a brief survey of the present position on our third centre of interest, transplantations from dead bodies, may show the contrary. Removal of organs from a deceased person is governed by the Human Tissue Act 1961, and this short Act of four sections had not been in operation very long before the new possibility of transplanting kidneys if removed quickly enough caused two government committees to be set up, and proposals were made in 1969 for the re-drafting of the Act (MacLennan, 1969). The Act distinguishes the rare cases in which the deceased has requested use of his body for medical purposes from the usual case in which the deceased has recorded no preference. Even so, where a request has been expressed, it will not necessarily prevail. Section 1(1) of the Act provides that

> if any person, either in writing at any time or orally in the presence of two or more witnesses during his last illness, has expressed a request that his body or any specified part of his body be used after his death for therapeutic purposes or for purposes of medical education or research, the person lawfully in possession of his body after his death may, unless he has reason to believe that the request was subsequently withdrawn, authorise the removal from the body of any part or, as the case may be, the specified part, for use in accordance with the request.

The expression "the person lawfully in possession of his body" is not defined and the concept continues to suffer from the uncertainty that attached to it under the pre-1961 law. It probably means the person who is under a duty to dispose of the body, and hospitals readily assume the rôle of being in possession of the body under pressure to act speedily while organs remain suitable for removal and transplantation. Whatever the expression may mean, however, such person only "may" authorize the removal; the section does not provide that he "must" do so, and the donor card scheme introduced in 1972 imposes on that person no duty to give his authorization.

Where, as is usual, no request has been made, section 1(2) enacts that

> the person lawfully in possession of the body of a deceased person may authorise the removal of any part from the body for use for the said purpose, if, having made such reasonable enquiry as may be practicable, he has no reason to believe—
>
> (a) that the deceased had expressed an objection to his body being so dealt with after his death, and had not withdrawn it; or
> (b) that the surviving spouse or any surviving relative of the deceased objects to the body being so dealt with.

What constitutes "such reasonable enquiry as may be practicable" must depend upon all of the circumstances, but because of the need to apply the provisions of this section at great speed, hospitals and coroners face the dilemma of either giving those words a demanding meaning, and losing transplant opportunities and no doubt patients' lives, or making them so easily satisfied as to render them meaningless, thereby denying the benefit of the Act to those whose sensibilities it is designed to protect. Moreover, when an enquiry is being made, the questions arise among the surviving spouse and relatives of remoteness and priority. Need, for instance, a second cousin by marriage be consulted, and if he is, will his objection overcome the consent to organ removal given by the spouse? The section requires only a "reasonable enquiry" but the absence of objection by "any surviving relative" is also necessary. In the absence of judicial interpretation it is not certain that the way in which hospitals at present apply the Act is in accordance with its true legal meaning, even if the apparent legal meaning itself is open to criticism for being unrealistic.

The Act also raises an absolutely fundamental legal problem in providing in section 1(4) that

> no such removal shall be effected except by a fully registered medical practitioner, who must have satisfied himself by personal examination of the body that life is extinct.

The legal test of extinction of life has become a matter of great controversy, because the law is inclined to see death as an event and not as a process, whereas it has been observed, in a terrible phrase, that "biologically we die in bits and pieces" (Shapiro, 1967). An invidious distinction is becoming apparent between "legal" death and "medical" or "clinical" death. The real question is really the stage in the process of dying at which organs can legally be removed for transplantation. The indications of death traditionally recognized in law are the absence of pulse and respiration, but now the medical concept has arisen of the decisive nature of "brain death", causing doctors to treat a patient as dead if his brain is damaged beyond prospect of recovering consciousness.

A patient whose breathing has stopped may be resuscitated and a heart that has stopped may be restarted, the patient recovering fully, provided that no brain damage has occurred, for instance by lack of oxygen supplied by the functions of breathing and blood circulation. On the other hand continuation of breathing and heartbeat will be discounted medically if there is no spark of activity in the brain that gives the body its human animation. The law is slow to adjust to this new test, however, and might not tolerate an operation to remove an organ from a respiring and pulsating body, even though these functions are being mechanically maintained when the brain is dead in order to preserve the organs for transplantation.

It may be feared that in this area of defining death the law has no clear answers at present, and may not even be asking the right questions about the nature of the life that is or is not extinct. This issue seems to lead on to our final topic, the mechanical prolongation of life.

MECHANICAL PROLONGATION OF LIFE

Legal difficulties in the mechanical prolongation of life are shown in a case occurring in 1963, *R. v. Potter* [13]. The accused was tried for assault after causing severe head injury when fighting with his victim. The victim was taken to hospital, and stopped breathing after fourteen hours. He was then maintained on an artificial respirator for twenty-four hours, after which, with the consent of his wife and a coroner, a kidney was removed for transplantation. The respirator was then shut off and the victim was found to have no spontaneous respiration or circulation. If we apply to these circumstances the orthodox legal test of life, that is breathing and heartbeat, the victim was alive until the machine was turned off. Two serious legal consequences follow from this. First, the kidney was removed from a living patient without his express or implied consent, constituting the crime of malicious wounding and the civil wrong of battery committed by the doctor responsible for the removal. Second, the doctor turning off the respirator caused the patient's death, and not the original assailant. In fact the Director of Public Prosecutions seems to have taken this view, because the accused was charged on his advice with only common assault, of which he was convicted, and not with manslaughter. This, of course, raises the issue of the doctor's legal liability for the death.

There have been no judicial decisions on medical liability for refusing to give or to continue to give mechanical support to a life that would end without it. Nevertheless, it seems in principle (Kennedy, 1969; Dworkin, 1970) that the courts would distinguish between the legal duty to give every patient "ordinary care", and medical discretion over "extraordinary care". "Ordinary care" appears to mean nursing care, food and drugs, and these cannot lawfully be withheld. In addition, drugs cannot be given with the intention that the patient shall die, however well-intentioned the doctor may be; the law does not recognize euthanasia. As medical techniques and resources improve, what was once "extraordinary care" may, of course, become "ordinary", and it is a matter of judgment whether a particular treatment has yet moved into the "ordinary" category. It may be believed that resuscitation is now "ordinary care", but not constantly repeated resuscitation when the patient has no hope of spontaneous recovery. Similarly, the economic fact of scarcity of machines to maintain respiration and heartbeat almost certainly leaves their use in the "extraordinary care" category, so that doctors have no legal duty to use them when they are available, and incur no legal liability in turning them off once they have been employed.

The scope of medical discretion may raise the natural fear that patients may be artificially kept alive until such time as doctors find it convenient to take out their organs for transplantation, and this has led to the recommendation by the Advisory Group on Transplantation Problems (MacLennan, 1969) that the decision to continue or discontinue artificial supports to life should be reached by doctors not involved in the possibility of a transplant. This recommendation has not yet been enacted by Parliament and, as in so many areas that have been touched on in this paper, there may be an unfortunate incompatibility between the requirements of the law and the demands of conscientious medical practice. Indeed, at times of despair it appears that the law, very inclined to look backwards to its first principles, and medical science, looking forward to a future the law cannot imagine, agree upon only one point; that a man cannot live for ever.

References

Abel-Smith, B. and Stevens, R. (1967). *Lawyers and the Courts.* London: Heinemann.

Bartholomew, G. W. (1958). Legal implications of artificial insemination. *Modern Law Review,* **236.**

Bevan, H. K. (1973). *The Law Relating to Children.* London: Butterworths.

Dworkin, G. (1970). The law relating to organ transplantation in England. *Modern Law Review,* **353.**

Edwards, J. Ll. J. (1964). *The Law Officers of the Crown.* London: Sweet and Maxwell.

Feversham, Lord (Chairman) (1960). *Report of the Departmental Committee on Human Artificial Insemination.* London: H.M.S.O. Cmnd. 1105.

Jackson, R. M. (1972). *The Machinery of Justice in England* (6th Edition) London: Cambridge University Press.

Kennedy, I. McC. (1969). Alive or dead? The lawyer's view. *Current Legal Problems,* **102.**

Kennedy, I. McC. (1973). The legal definition of death. *Medico-Legal Journal,* **36.**

Kleegman, S. J. and Kaufman, S. A. (1966). *Infertility in Women.* Philadelphia: F. A. Davis.

Leach, G. (1972). *The Biocrats.* Harmondsworth: Penguin Books.

MacLennan, H. (Chairman) (1969). *Advice from the Advisory Group on Transplantation Problems.* London: H.M.S.O. Cmnd. 4106.

Meyers, D. W. (1970). *The Human Body and the Law.* Edinburgh: Edinburgh University Press.

Shapiro, H. A. (1967). Organ grafting in man. *Journal of Forensic Medicine,* **41.**

Stevas, N. St. J. (1961). *Life, Death and the Law.* London: Eyre and Spottiswoode.

Titmuss, R. M. (1971). *The Gift Relationship.* London: Allen and Unwin.

Williams, G. (1958). *The Sanctity of Life and the Criminal Law.* London: Faber and Faber.

Williams, G. (1962). Consent and public policy. *Criminal Law Review,* **74, 154.**

Legal References

1. *R. v. Bourne* [1939] 1 K.B. 687; [1938] 3 All E.R. 615.
2. 1958 S.L.T. 12.
3. *Bravery v. Bravery* [1954] 3 All E.R. 59 at pp. 67–8.
4. *R. v. Coney* (1882) 8 Q.B.D. 534.
5. *R. v. Donovan* [1934] 2 K.B. 498.
6. *R. v. Wright* 1 Co. Lit. F. 127 A-B.
7. Lord Jowitt in *Baxter v. Baxter* [1948] A.C. 274 at p. 286.
8. Orde J. (1921) 49 Ontario L.R. 15 at p. 22; and see Lord Dunedin in *Russell v. Russell* [1924] A.C. 687 at p. 721.
9. *Ibid.* at p. 23.
10. *R. v. Poulton* (1832) 5 C. & P. 329, *R. v. Sellis* (1837) 7 C. & P. 850.
11. *R. v. Enoch* (1833) 5 C. & P. 539, *R. v. Wright* (1841) 9 C. & P. 754.
12. s. 4(2); and see Macnaghten J. in *R. v. Bourne* [1938] 3 All E.R. 615 at p. 620.
13. (1963) 31 Medico-Legal Journal 195; and see (1964) 4 Medicine, Science and the Law pp. 59 and 77.

New Biology—New Ethics

ELIOT SLATER

Institute of Psychiatry, University of London, London England

It is often maintained that "science is science" in the same kind of way as "business is business". There is no room for moral values or ethical concepts in the scientist's equations or the businessman's balance sheets. Let them intrude even into the background thinking and, they say, it would lead to confusion. These are all different universes of discourse; and the necessary concepts of the one may be meaningless in the other context. This is true; but I wish to submit that it is only part of the truth.

In the world of physical reality if we want to find the truth we must put into cold storage ideas of what we should like to be the truth. To quote Bertrand Russell (1954):

> Ethical considerations can only legitimately appear when the truth has been ascertained: they can and should appear as determining our feelings towards the truth, and our manner of ordering our lives in view of the truth, but not as themselves dictating what the truth shall be.

Russell's principle directs us to examine in a dispassionate way all manner of problems with a factual basis, whatever their emotional repercussions. There is no reason why the principle should not apply in other worlds than that of physical reality, e.g. in the social sciences, that is, as long as there *is* a truth that can be ascertained. If we had the self-discipline to follow Russell here, we might make progress towards understanding such things as racial problems, sex deviations, drug addiction, violence, and the containment of social evils. If we did not feel so strongly, we might think more clearly.

However, scientific indifferentism has dangers of its own. After the clear thinking, dispassionate enquiry and cool understanding there comes action, or a decision not to act. When we act, or refrain from acting, it is out of our subjectivities, dominated by wishes and fears,

177

mental habits and mental inertia, all set against standards of value. In fact, everything we do has an ethical dimension. If we make the amoralism, which is appropriate to factual enquiries, into such a habit of mind that it pervades the life of action, we become dehumanized. All intellectual workers run this risk, not only in science, but notably also in law, administration and commerce. On the grand scale, the divorce of factual from ethical thinking contributes to the growth of global dangers. At the individual level it leads to a petrification of the personality. The scientist should not feel it open to him to make a career out of the study of neurotoxic gases, or to pursue the truth by way of cruel experiments on animals, or to act as if his only concern was what is going on at the laboratory bench.

One fundamental cause of danger to the scientist comes from an instrumentalist philosophy of knowledge. This is an epistemological school which has been vigorously combated by Karl Popper, perhaps in vain. Instrumentalism is a way of evading basic difficulties, and it seems to be necessary because reality, from the cosmos to the microcosm, has become impenetrable to an understanding armed only with familiar models and images. It is only a Euclidean geometry that we can understand instinctively; curved space-time is not something we can feel in our bones. The scientists who concern themselves with the mythic entities of modern physics have given up model-making. All that is necessary for research to proceed is for the problem to be expressed in the appropriate mathematical language. We may give them names, the neutrino, the quark and the tachyon, but to define and describe them other symbols than words are required. Translation from one language to the other is both unnecessary and impossible. They are, then, incomprehensible in any ordinary sense. But instrumentalism enables us to work with familiarity with concepts we do not even try to understand.

The immense prestige of physics leads to a similar approach becoming more and more the chosen philosophy of the life sciences. Information is sought not so much for imaginative understanding as for the capacity to make predictions and to manipulate material to attain desired ends. A line of mouse-human hybrid cells can be submitted to question in the same spirit of dispassionate ruthlessness as inanimate nature. And so, in turn, can the mice. And the humans. The human experimental subject becomes just another black box, capable indeed of verbal behaviour, but none the less amenable to the constraints of behaviouristic experiment. The ethical dimension becomes invisible.

But there are ancient gods who stand guard over the way from the temple of Truth to the public forum, from the understanding of a problem to its practical solution. Categorical imperatives and prohibitions rear up on every side. Simple solutions that nature provides are held to be ethically unacceptable. If a primitive people can lead a stable existence in harmony with its environment by means of tribal warfare, head-hunting, cannibalism and infanticide, from where do we get the right to intervene? Can we honestly claim that our ethics are better?

It is unthinkable—now—that the world should cope with overpopulation by licensed infanticide. Infanticide is sporadically but universally practised, and is universally forbidden. However, when we deny ourselves the easy ways, it is usually possible to do something the hard way. If a contraceptive were found specifically lethal to the XX gamete, I have no doubt but that it would be thought ethically acceptable. Oriental societies could regulate their families to produce sons only, with social consequences incalculable and almost certainly disastrous.

It is usually possible to get on the blind side of the gods; and one way to avoid those terrible commands and prohibitions is by redefinitions which take a problem beyond their scope. For instance, is a man really alive whose spirit has departed from him, who by brain injury or brain disease has lost even the knowledge of his own identity? It would be good instrumentalist epistemology to regard the hulk that remains as already dead. At the humane level it would be kind to the relatives, and kind also to a generation of elderly people who envisage the possibility of a fate worse than death. Perhaps one might even add that it would tend to relieve the strains on our overstressed hospital services; and that it might divert scientific effort unprofitably spent on the problems of ageing to more worth-while fields.

We seem recently to have got rather confused about what constitutes a human being. While normal embryos are not held to have attained this status, it has been allowed to mistakes of nature that reach birth and survive into a future for ever incapable of independent existence. It should not be too difficult for us to categorize anencephalic newborns as without human potentiality, permitting ourselves to put them down without further ado. And if so with the anencephalics, why not so also with other examples of hopelessly defective quasi-human machinery? Genetic engineering to correct a genic defect so easily eliminated by nature's own methods might at least be given the tests of cost-benefit analysis, if our new biology is to conform to any rational ethics.

Theistic religions have now almost completely broken down in the Western world. But law and administration are still governed by the vestiges of a Judaeo-Christian morality. For very large organizational systems have an immense inertia. Nevertheless, when universal convictions have eroded and dogma dies, the ethical values they supported can undergo revolutionary changes, even in a single generation. A shift in the balance of opinion in the educated middle classes led to abortion law reform; and the change in the law triggered off a transformation of medical ethics and medical practice. We are now witnessing a change in informed opinion about euthanasia; and there too the switch effect of a change in the law might open a floodgate to social change. Bit by bit the Christian ethic gives way to an irreligious humanitarianism. As old inhibitions are dissipated, new freedoms arise and new possibilities of welfare or ruin.

The instability of the social system, and the possibilities of a violent swing in one or another direction, will presumably become even greater as the decay of humanism follows the decay of theisms. Mankind has unfortunately come to recognize itself as overwhelmingly the most important global pest species, as much for itself as for the rest of the biosphere. Anything but cynicism about anthropocentric standards of value will become increasingly difficult. What will happen when we are freed from their inhibitions is beyond our guess.

We already need a new focus around which to centre our value systems. We might find it, not in ourselves, but in the planet which is in our guardianship. Mankind will surely bring itself to ruin, if it strives only for the welfare of mankind. Nothing prospers, neither the individual nor the group nor the institution, which gives its loyalty only to itself.

Strangely enough, this is a lesson taught us by the new biology, which shows us all organisms living in an ecology in which each has its part. If the inanimate world shows us no ethical dimension, we may find it in height and depth in the living world. It is a wisdom of nature, one might say, that requires each species to live not for itself alone.

Reference

Russell, Bertrand (1954). *Mysticism and Logic*. London: Penguin Books.

Index